This book belongs to

....

....

....

For Ian
Best, Britta xxx
B. T.

For Seren and Scarlett,
with much love from Fiona
F. M. W.

Tiger, Tiger, Burning Bright! gathers poems from all over the world.
Regional spellings and usage have been retained in order to preserve the integrity of the originals.

First published 2020 by Nosy Crow Ltd
The Crow's Nest, 14 Baden Place, Crosby Row, London SE1 1YW
www.nosycrow.com

ISBN 978 1 78800 567 8

This book is published by Nosy Crow in collaboration with the National Trust
nationaltrust.org.uk/books.
'The National Trust' and the oak leaf logo are registered trademarks of The National Trust
(Enterprises) Limited (a subsidiary of the National Trust for Places of Historic Interest or
Natural Beauty, Registered Charity Number 205846).
Nosy Crow and associated logos are trademarks and/or registered trademarks of Nosy Crow Ltd.

This selection © Fiona Waters 2020
Illustrations © Britta Teckentrup 2020

Copyright © of poems, and First Nations Australian cultural material, remains with its creators.
"Paddling, we saw that turtle" on page 96 used with permission from Buku-Larrnggay Mulka Centre
on behalf of Rirratjiŋu clan, Yolŋu people, North East Arnhem Land, Northern Territory, Australia.
The editor and publisher claim no ownership over First Nations Australian cultural material referenced
in the book, and received permission for its use. Please contact the publisher with any concerns.

The acknowledgements on pages 323–325 constitute an extension of this copyright page.

The right of Fiona Waters to be identified as the compiler and Britta Teckentrup
to be identified as the illustrator of this work has been asserted.
All rights reserved.

A CIP catalogue record for this book is available from the British Library.

Printed in China
Papers used by Nosy Crow are made from wood grown in responsible forests.

MIX
Paper from
responsible sources
FSC® C010256
www.fsc.org

10 9 8 7 6 5 4 3 2 1

TIGER, TIGER, BURNING BRIGHT!

selected by
Fiona Waters

illustrated by
Britta Teckentrup

nosy crow

CONTENTS

INTRODUCTION

I am lucky enough to edit picture books for young children for my living. I dream about stories, beginnings, middles and endings, and love how words and pictures work together brilliantly to tell a tale. The very best books of all make my heart sing and my skin tingle.

But . . . I think I might be quite a poetry person, too. As a child, I missed a year of school due to illness, and a kindly and inspirational teacher (Ms Gaskell, thank you) gave me bags and bags of books. Up until then, I mainly trailed after my older brother and sister, but those bags of books made a bookworm of me. When I was better, I was allowed to walk to the tiny village library on my own and found not just more stories but poetry, too. I loved the reassuring rhythms – they were so beautifully predictable – and I liked the way a poem could look. The words didn't fill all the white but left funny spaces, as if to give me room to think. My favourite collection was my mum's beloved *Albatross Book of Verse*. At seven, I didn't always understand very much, but Ms Gaskell said that was OK; she said it was "the reading that mattered".

The reading really did matter and here we are, many years later. I've learnt so much about words and pictures and meanings and now see how poems and picture books are so very similar. Picture books, as a wise person once said, should be both windows and mirrors: they enable children to see out into other worlds whilst also reflecting their own. They provide comfort or reassurance or sometimes just good old entertainment, or maybe a combination of many things. A poem does all of this, too. Look at how a tiny collection of words, carefully arranged, can say so much. Poems are bite-size, mini-story worlds that can be nibbled upon word by word or just swallowed whole in one big gulp. And, like a picture book, a poem always, always makes us feel something.

When we were thinking about ideas for this book, we talked about the funny spaces that poems leave on the page and how pictures can make a poem so much more. We also thought about the things that children really love and what poems might appeal to them. I thought about my son, who at the age of three, was in love with his encyclopedia of animals. It was almost bigger than him and had hundreds of pictures of nearly every animal you could think of.

So, why not a poetry anthology that was all about animals? A glorious collection of as many animal poems that we could find, with one poem for every day of the year, that a child (or parent or uncle or carer or friend) could dip in and out of as they pleased. And this felt like a very important decision. Poems and reading "matter" more than ever but so does the natural world. If this book can nurture a love of the animal kingdom, then maybe it will also help create the conservationists of the future.

Fiona, the anthologist, has found wonderful poems for you to enjoy, and Britta, the artist, has created a beautiful visual story on every page. There are poems to make you think, poems to make you laugh, poems that you'll want to share and some that will stay with you forever. There are some poems that you might know already, but hopefully you'll make lots of exciting new discoveries, too. You might find that there are some you would like to go back to. And perhaps that poem will say a different thing on a different day. Remember that you don't always have to understand a poem. Poems are like that.

And just as there are all sorts of poems, there are all sorts of creatures here, too. Sometimes our job wasn't easy – it's quite hard to find a poem about an aardvark! – but we think that there are enough species here to fill the ark, from the crabs on Christmas Island to migrating monarch butterflies, the splendour of an Indian elephant and, of course, plenty of dogs and cats and lions and tigers and bears. There are also lots of unsung heroes – the humble snail, the tiny ant, the shy platypus. Who knows, maybe your favourite animal will appear on your birthday? Wouldn't that be nice?

I feel very proud to have helped make this book and hope that all the wonderful poems here might make your heart sing and your skin tingle, and make *you* a poetry person, too.

Louise Bolongaro
Head of Picture Books, Nosy Crow

JANUARY

1ST

POLAR CUB

This way, that way?
Step out,
little five-toe flat-foot,
squint-eye,
cave-dazed,
into the sun!

Eyes left,
ears right,
nose to the wind!

The coast is clear!
Run, roll, lollop;
winter's done!
Enjoy the pause;
make your mark
on this blank page—
the world is yours!

Judith Nicholls

2nd

THE CUB

Said the cub to his mother,
"Am I a Polar Bear?"
"Of course you are," she answered.
"There's your father standing there,
We all live in the Arctic,
Amidst the ice and snow,
And, if you were not a Polar Bear,
I'd be the first to know."

He said, "Could I be an Aadvark,
A fox or kangaroo?
Or perhaps I'm a gorilla,
A dog or shaggy gnu."
"Stop asking silly questions, son,
You're a bear as you've been told."
"Well, if I'm a Polar Bear," he said,
"Why do I feel so cold?"

Russell Hannah

3rd

THE POLAR BEAR

The polar bear's
fur is
like sugar.
His nose
is like a
black plum.

Jason Fields

4th

WHALE-CLOUD

You watch me in the sea Whale-cloud

I bathing in your world, you floating in mine

I stretch out my arms and legs, bob in the rolling water

On the wind you move east, a flick of your tail for speed

In bed, I rub salty feet together

While you cry Whale-cloud tears over parched farms somewhere far away

In sleep and play I forget you

But afternoon sun on my sandcastle reminds me to look up for you my friend

The wind has turned west

You are swimming back to me

S. J. Perillo

5th

WHALESONG

I am
ocean voyager,
sky-leaper,
maker of waves;
I harm no man.

I know
only the slow tune
of turning tide,
the heave and sigh
of full seas meeting land
at dusk and dawn,
the sad whale song.
I harm no man.

Judith Nicholls

6th

THE SHEEPDOG

After the very bright light,
And the talking bird,
And the singing,
And the sky filled up wi' wings,
And then the silence,

Our lads sez
We'd better go, then.
Stay, Shep. Good dog, stay.
So I stayed wi' t' sheep.

After they cum back,
It sounded grand, what they'd seen:
Camels, and kings, and such,
Wi' presents—human sort,
Not the kind you eat—
And a baby. Presents wes for him.
Our lads took him a lamb.

I had to stay behind wi' t' sheep.
Pity they didn't tek me along too.
I'm good wi' lambs,
And the baby might have liked a dog
After all that myrrh and such.

U. A. Fanthorpe

7th

GREY WOLF

I am the grey wolf
shadow on snow

I am the silence
of the high places

the dark of ancient forests
I am closer than you know

feel the steam of my breath
in this icy air

see the gleam
the amber lightning of my eye

between black pines
the pack gathers

I am the thunderhead
we are the coming storm

Jan Dean

8th

a marsh hawk
tips the solitary
pine

John Wills

9th

SONG OF AN OLD GRAY WOLF

The world is large and wide and long.
A great many wolves have been born in the world.
But I alone have been all over the world.
Today I am so old that at last my old age is over.

Cheyenne song,
translated by Alfred Kroeber

10th

MOTHER DOESN'T WANT A DOG

Mother doesn't want a dog.
Mother says they smell,
And never sit when you say sit,
Or even when you yell.
And when you come home late at night
And there is ice and snow,
You have to go back out because
The dumb dog has to go.

Mother doesn't want a dog.
Mother says they shed,
And always let the strangers in
And bark at friends instead,
And do disgraceful things on rugs,
And track mud on the floor,
And flop upon your bed at night
And snore their doggy snore.

Mother doesn't want a dog.
She's making a mistake.
Because, more than a dog, I think
She will not want this snake.

Judith Viorst

11th

A CHILD'S DREAM
(EXTRACT)

I had a little dog,
    and my dog was very small.
He licked me in the face,
    and he answered to my call.
Of all the treasures that were mine,
    I loved him best of all.

Frances Cornford

12th

THE DOG

The truth I do not stretch or shove
When I state the dog is full of love.
I've also proved, by actual test,
A wet dog is the lovingest.

Ogden Nash

13th

PENGUIN

This stone I set at your feet
As my courtship gift to you
At the white summer's end
On Antarctica's icy shore.

Later you lay your egg
And ease it on to my feet.
You turn and walk away,
Black going into the blackness.

I stand, Emperor of this land,
My back to the blistering wind,
Shifting my feet with care
Through the dark of sixty days.

Will you return as the egg hatches,
Fat, and with belly full to feed
Our young? Will you find us here
Amidst this blinding snow?

Yes, and I must now walk
My shrunken self the hundred icy
Miles to open sea, then, fattened,
The hundred back, my belly lardered.

And so through all the long dark
We trudge, or stand, under the howling sky.
In the fading summer I will bring again
The honest gift of a stone.

Michael Harrison

14th
THE HORSE

Standing lonely,
Like a bullied child.
Tied up in the corner,
He longs for the wild.

The soft black eyes,
Of his gentle face,
Seem warm and comforting,
In this cold dark place.

His muscles tense up,
As he takes the strain.
With a challenging rear,
He tears away from the chain.

Out into the night,
And away like a bird,
He gallops and gallops,
Until no more he is heard.

He looks like a picture,
As he flies over the ground,
With his neck outstretched,
Not making a sound.

A piercing whinny
Cuts through the night sky.
He stops dead in his tracks,
His head held up high.

Far in the distance
They come into sight,
Three galloping horses,
Two black and one white.

The horse, he stands watching,
This magnificent three.
Then as a foursome together,
They run to be free.

Laura Allen

15th
WINTER

In the night,
Came a white horse to visit.
His hooves made no sound
As he covered the ground,
And snow filled the land with its spirit.

Andrew Fusek Peters

16th

THE RED FOX

Have you heard her yipping
when the moon is down?

Have you seen her skipping
on the snow-coat hills?

The red fox dipping
her paintbrush paws
into the drifts she loves.

J. Patrick Lewis

17th

SONG OF THE RABBITS
OUTSIDE THE TAVERN

We who play under the pines,
we who dance in the snow
that shines blue in the light of the moon
sometimes halt as we go,
stand with our ears erect,
our noses testing the air,
to gaze at the golden world
behind the windows there.

Suns they have in a cave
and stars each on a tall white stem,
and the thought of fox or night owl
seems never to trouble them.
They laugh and eat and are warm,
their food seems ready at hand,
while hungry out in the cold
we little rabbits stand.

But they never dance as we dance,
they have not the speed nor the grace.
We scorn both the cat and the dog
who lie by their fireplace.
We scorn them licking their paws,
their eyes on an upraised spoon,
we who dance hungry and wild
under a winter's moon.

Elizabeth Coatsworth

18th

In the winter storm
The cat keeps on
Blinking its eyes.

Saijō Yaso,
translated by R. H. Blyth

19th

WINTER DUCKS

Small in the shrink of winter, dark of the frost and chill,
Dawnlight beyond my windowsill,
I lace the morning stiffly on my feet,
Print bootsteps down the snowy hill to meet
My ducks all waiting where the long black night
Has iced the pond around them. With a spade
I break the water clear; the hole I made
Restores their world to quacking rhyme and reason—
Tails up, they duck the lowering, grey-skied season,
Heads down, they listen to the still-warm song
Of silted leaves and summer, when the days were long.

Russell Hoban

20th

A grey morning
     ducks whistle down
to skid on ice

Colin Oliver

21st

Perfectly still
in the falling snow
grey heron

Roberta Davis

22nd

THE PUFFIN

Upon this cake of ice is perched
The paddle-footed Puffin;
To find his double we have searched,
But have discovered—Nuffin!

Robert Williams Wood

23rd

BIRD SONG
(EXTRACT)

The great gull hovers
on wings spread wide
above us, above us.
He stares, I shout!
His head is white,
his beak gapes,
his small round eyes
look far, look sharp!
        Qutiuk! Qutiuk!

The great skua hovers
on wings spread wide
above us, above us.
He stares, I shout!
His head is black,
his beak gapes,
his small round eyes
look far, look sharp!
        Ijoq! Ijoq!

Inuit song,
translated by Tom Lowenstein

24th

AN AUK IN FLIGHT

An auk in flight
is sheer delight,
it soars above the sea.

An auk on land
is not so grand—
an auk walks **auk**wardly.

Jack Prelutsky

25th

THE SEAGULL

Seagull, seagull, sit on the sand,
It's never good weather when you're on the land.

Anonymous

26th

FISHES

Fishes
Tiny, shiny
Flashing, dashing, diving
Glimpses of ocean mystery
Teasers

Kate Williams

27th

CROSS PORPOISES

The porpoises
were looking really cross
so I went over
and talked at them

Soon they cheered up
and swam away
leaving laughter-bubbles
in their wake

It never fails,
talking at cross porpoises.

Roger McGough

28th

THE SEA

Behold the wonders of the mighty deep,
Where crabs and lobsters learn to creep,
And little fishes learn to swim,
And clumsy sailors tumble in.

Anonymous

29th

CAT BEGAN

Cat began.
She took the howling of the wind,
She took the screeching of the owl
And made her voice.

For her coat
She took the softness of the snow,
She took the yellow of the sand,
She took the shadows of the branches of the trees.

From deep wells
She took the silences of stones,
She took the moving of the water
For her walk.

Then at night
Cat took the glittering of stars,
She took the blackness of the sky
To make her eyes.

Fire and ice
Went in the sharpness of her claws
And for their shape
She took the new moon's slender curve—

And Cat was made.

Andrew Matthews

30th

CAT

The black cat yawns,
Opens her jaws,
Stretches her legs,
And shows her claws.

Then she gets up
And stands on four
Long stiff legs
And yawns some more.

She shows her sharp teeth,
She stretches her lip,
Her slice of a tongue
Turns up at the tip.

Lifting herself
On her delicate toes,
She arches her back
As high as it goes.

She lets herself down
With particular care,
And pads away
With her tail in the air.

Mary B. Miller

31st

THE TIGER

Tiger! Tiger! burning bright
In the forests of the night,
What immortal hand or eye
Could frame thy fearful symmetry?

In what distant deeps or skies
Burnt the fire of thine eyes?
On what wings dare he aspire?
What the hand dare seize the fire?

And what shoulder, and what art,
Could twist the sinews of thy heart?
And when thy heart began to beat,
What dread hand? and what dread feet?

What the hammer? what the chain?
In what furnace was thy brain?
What the anvil? what dread grasp
Dare its deadly terrors clasp?

When the stars threw down their spears,
And watered heaven with their tears,
Did he smile his work to see?
Did he who made the Lamb make thee?

Tiger! Tiger! burning bright
In the forests of the night,
What immortal hand or eye
Dare frame thy fearful symmetry?

William Blake

FEBRUARY

1st

GRANDPA BEAR'S LULLABY

The night is long
But fur is deep.
You will be warm
In winter sleep.

The food is gone
But dreams are sweet
And they will be
Your winter meat.

The cave is dark
But dreams are bright
And they will serve
As winter light.
Sleep, my little cubs, sleep.

Jane Yolen

2nd

GROUND HOG DAY

Ground Hog sleeps
All winter
Snug in his fur,
Dreams
Green dreams of
Grassy shoots,
Of nicely newly nibbly
Roots—
Ah, he starts to
Stir.
With drowsy
Stare
Looks from his burrow
Out on fields of
Snow.
What's there?
Oh no.
His shadow. Oh,
How sad!
Six more
Wintry
Weeks
To go.

Lilian Moore

3rd

HOW MUCH WOOD WOULD A WOODCHUCK CHUCK

How much wood would a woodchuck chuck
If a woodchuck could chuck wood?
He would chuck as much wood as a woodchuck would chuck,
If a woodchuck could chuck wood.

Anonymous

4th

SNOW LEOPARD

She casts
dark shades
of black
on white,
as fresh
fine snow
falls to
the ground.
She creeps,
in stealth,
to hunt
her prey
in still
black of
night, then
sleeps sound
by light
of day.
Her world
is cold,
as she
grows old.
Paw prints
sight, black
on white.

Connie Marcum Wong

5th

SNOW LEOPARD HAIKU

Fluffy and sharp claws
Soft and warm, cold, rough noses
Sharp teeth, spotty, WILD!

Lucy-Beth Cassidy

6th

THE BLUE BIRD

At the foot of the cliff
On the face of the cliff
The blue bird sings

Southern Paiute song,
translated by John Wesley Powell

7th

I WATCHED AN EAGLE SOAR

Grandmother,
I watched an eagle soar
high in the sky
until a cloud covered him up.
Grandmother,
I still saw the eagle
behind my eyes.

Virginia Driving Hawk Sneve

8th

MICHAEL'S SONG

Because I set no snare
But leave them flying free,
All the birds of the air
Belong to me.

From the blue tit on the sloe
To the eagle on the height
Uncaged they come and go
For my delight.

And so the sunward way
I soar on the eagle's wings,
And in my heart all day
The blue tit sings.

Wilfrid Gibson

9th

THE WOLF CRY

The Arctic moon hangs overhead;
The wide white silence lies below.
A starveling pine stands lone and gaunt,
Black-penciled on the snow.

Weird as the moan of sobbing winds,
A lone long call floats up from the trail;
And the naked soul of the frozen North
Trembles in that wail.

Lew Sarett

10th

THE SNOW-SHOE HARE

The Snow-shoe Hare
Is his own sudden blizzard.

Or he comes, limping after the snow storm,
A big, lost, left-behind snowflake
Crippled with bandages.

White, he is looking for a great whiteness
To hide in.
But the starry night is on his track.

His own dogged shadow
Panics him to right, then to left, then backwards,
Then forwards—
Till he skids skittering
Out across the blue ice, meeting the Moon.

He stretches up, craning slender
Listening
For the Fox's icicles and the White Owl's frore cloud.

In his popping eyes
The whole crowded heaven struggles softly.

Glassy mountains, breathless, brittle forests
Are frosty aerials
Balanced in his ears.

And his nose bobs wilder
And his heart thuds harder

Tethered there, so hotly
To his crouching shadow.

Ted Hughes

11th

THE ANACONDA

The anaconda stretches a long long long long way—Its head is in tomorrow, while its tail's still in today.

Richard Edwards

12th

THE CENTIPEDE'S DILEMMA

A centipede was happy quite
Until a frog in fun
Said, "Pray, which leg comes after which?"
This raised her mind to such a pitch,
She lay distracted in a ditch,
Considering how to run.

Katherine Craster

13th

IGUANA MEMORY

Saw an iguana once
when I was very small
in our backdam backyard
came rustling across my path

green like moving newleaf sunlight

big like big big lizard
with more legs than centipede
so it seemed to me
and it must have stopped a while
eyes meeting mine
iguana and child locked in a brief
split moment happening
before it went hurrying

    for the green of its life

Grace Nichols

14th

PORCUPINE VALENTINE

Porcupine, oh Porcupine,
Will you be my Valentine?
The touch of your quills sends chills down my spines.
My heart skips a beat whenever we meet.
I love the way you start to rattle
When you stamp your tiny feet.
I adore your sharp claws,
I pine for your spines.
Please be mine,
Porcupine
Valentine.

Jane Clarke

15th

There were two skunks—
Out and In.
When In was out,
Out was in.
One day Out was in and In was out.
Their mother,
who was in with Out,
wanted In in.
"Bring In in,"
she said to Out.
So Out went out
and brought In in.
"How did you find him
so fast?" she asked.
"Instinct," he said.

Anonymous

16th

THE KANGAROO

Water beneath the hills,
running slowly from the creek,
towards the hills.

Birds sitting on the branch,
smelling the red flowers
that are growing.

Kangaroo is lying in the shade,
very tired from hopping around,
he listens to the water,
that is running very slowly.

He is happy, no people around,
to spear him.
He smells the red flowers,
so tired he goes to sleep.

Pansy Rose Napaljarri

17th

THE PLATYPUS

My child, the Duck-billed Platypus
A sad example sets for us:
From him we learn how Indecision
Of character provokes Derision.
This vacillating Thing, you see,
Could not decide which he would be,
Fish, Flesh or Fowl, and chose all three.
The scientists were sorely vexed
To classify him; so perplexed
Their brains, that they, with Rage at bay,
Called him a horrid name one day,—
A name that baffles, frights and shocks us,
Ornithorhynchus Paradoxus.

Oliver Herford

18th

PLATYPUS

Some of us
Still wonder at the platypus.
Is he a duck
That is out of luck?
Or a mole
That has lost its hole?
He would have been a tasty dish
If he was a fish.
He is stubborn and strong-willed
And strongly billed
As every burrower's wish.

Faustin Charles

19th

EVERY INSECT

Every Insect (ant, fly, bee)
Is divided into three:
One head, one chest, one stomach part.

Some have brains.
All have a heart.

Insects have no bones,

No noses.

But with feelers they can smell
Dinner half a mile away.

Can your nose do half as well?

Also you'd be in a fix
With all those legs to manage:
Six.

Dorothy Aldis

20th

THE ANT

The ant has made himself illustrious
Through constant industry industrious.
So what?
Would you be calm and placid
If you were full of formic acid?

Ogden Nash

21st

ANTEATER

Anteater, Anteater
Where have you been?
Aunt Liz took you walkies
And hasn't been seen.

Nor has Aunt Mary,
Aunt Flo or Aunt Di.
Anteater, Anteater
Why the gleam in your eye?

S. K. Werp

22nd

ANTEATER

Imagine overturning
The teeming anthill
Without a qualm,
Calmly sweeping
Up its angry
Inhabitants on a
Long sticky tongue,
And swallowing the
Lot with relish—
As if those
Beady little bodies
Made just so many
Mouthfuls of red
Or black caviar.

Valerie Worth

23rd

OUR NIGHT OWL

Through the tracery of trees
of a winter night
black beyond twilight
on luminous sky
an owl hoots here hoots there hoots where
a will'o the wisp
wild above the village
the warm lit windows
the frosty lanes
the ancient streams
pinched into running drains
above the muntjac's
raucous rasp
the TV sets
and muffled ears.

Sheila Paine

24th

PIGEONS

On shallow slates the pigeons shift together,
Backing against a thin rain from the west
Blown across each sunk head and settled feather.
Huddling round the warm stack suits them best,
Till winter daylight weakens, and they grow
Hardly defined against the brickwork. Soon,
Light from a small intense lopsided moon
Shows them, black as their shadows, sleeping so.

Philip Larkin

25th

Bleak midwinter—
on the bare oak branch
a sparrow see-saws

Cy Patterson

59

26th

BABY ORANGUTAN

Bold flare of orange—
a struck match
against his mother's breast

he listens to her heartbeat
going yes yes yes

Helen Dunmore

27th

FIRST SIGHT

Lambs that learn to walk in snow
When their bleating clouds the air
Meet a vast unwelcome, know
Nothing but a sunless glare.
Newly stumbling to and fro
All they find, outside the fold
Is a wretched width of cold.

As they wait beside the ewe,
Her fleeces wetly caked, there lies
Hidden round them, waiting too,
Earth's immeasurable surprise.
They could not grasp it if they knew,
What so soon will wake and grow
Utterly unlike the snow.

Philip Larkin

28th

BAA, BAA, BLACK SHEEP

Baa, baa, black sheep,
Have you any wool?
Yes, sir; yes, sir—
Three bags full.

One for the master,
One for the dame;
One for the little boy
Who lives down the lane.

Anonymous

29th

THE SHEEP'S CONFESSION

I look stupid, much like a dirty heap of snow
The Winter left.
I have nothing to draw your attention, nothing for show,
Except the craft

Which shears me and leaves me looking even more
Unintelligent.
I do not wonder you laugh when you see my bare
Flesh like a tent

Whose guy-ropes broke. But listen, I have one thing
To charm and delight –
The lamb I drop when Winter is turning to Spring.
His coat is white,

Purer than mine and he wears socks of black wool.
He can move
And prance. I am proud of a son so beautiful
And so worthy of love.

Elizabeth Jennings

MARCH

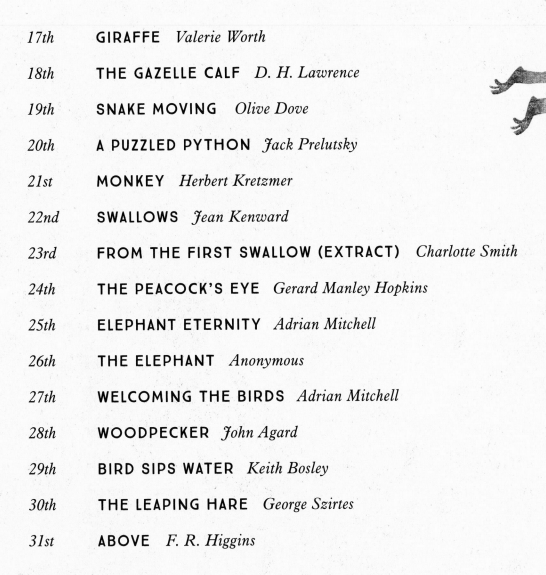

1st

WHO AM I?

As black as ink and isn't ink,
As white as milk and isn't milk,
As soft as silk and isn't silk,
And hops about like a filly-foal.

[A magpie]

Anonymous

2nd

MARCH

A blue day,
a blue jay
and a good beginning.

One crow,
melting snow—
spring's winning!

Elizabeth Coatsworth

3rd

MURDER OF CROWS

We're the best dressed here.
Forget the scruffy starlings
dishevelled thrushes
the gaudy tits and finches—
they're all a waste of space.

We're the real class act:
never a feather out of place
our blacks perfectly matched.
Like gangsters, ministers,
we demand respect.

Our quills drink in the light
like ink.

Dilys Rose

4th

SPIDERWEB

From other
angles the
fibers look
fragile, but
not from the
spider's, always
hauling coarse
ropes, hitching
lines to the
best posts
possible. It's
heavy work
everyplace,
fighting sag,
winching up
give. It
isn't ever
delicate
to live.

Kay Ryan

5th

A FLY

If I could
See this fly
With unprejudiced eye,
I should see his body
Was metallic blue—no,
Peacock blue.
His wings are a frosty puff;
His legs fine wire.
He even has a face,
I notice.
And he breathes as I do.

Ruth Dallas

6th

SPIDER

I'm told that the spider
Has coiled up inside her
Enough silky material
To spin an aerial
One-way track
To the moon and back;
Whilst I
Cannot even catch a fly.

Frank Collymore

7th

HOW TO BE A MOLE

Make your home
in the damp darkness
underground
unknowing of snow
and stars
and summer breezes.
Live among roots
and rocks
and sleeping cicadas.
Excavate tunnels
in the moist brown earth.
Listen for the soft music
of seeds sprouting,
worms wiggling,
rain pattering on your grassy roof.
Spend your days in a world
of unending night.

Elaine Magliaro

8th

MY GARDEN

Rabbits and moles
Always make holes.

It's a rabbit habit.

But the moles should be told
That my lawn is all-holed.

Barbara Ireson

9th

RABBIT'S SPRING

Snow
Goes,

Ice
Thaws,

Warm
Paws!

Brian Patten

10th

AWAKE, ASLEEP

Awake from hibernation
The bear nosed through the wood,
Ate bulbs and roots and snails—
Everything tasted good,
Ate shoots and fruits and wasp nests,
Ate ants' eggs for a treat,
Ate cranberries, bilberries, crowberries—
Everything tasted sweet.

Awake from hibernation,
The bear nosed through the trees,
Ate salmon from the rivers,
Ate honey from the bees,
Ate till the leaves turned rusty
And the cold mists swirled,
Came to a cave, remembered,
And vanished from the world.

Richard Edwards

11th

THE CROW

Flying loose and easy, where does he go
Swaggering in the sky, what does he know,
Why is he laughing, the carrion crow?
Why is he shouting, why won't he sing,
How did he steal them, whom will he bring
Loaves of blue heaven under each wing?

Russell Hoban

12th

BIG BLACK BEAR

Big black bear
Hiding in his shadow

Steve Meadows

13th

TROTTING, TROTTING, TROTTING
INTO THE DUSK AND HOME

A dog is trotting home;
Trotting on a long unending beach,
Trotting
Just where the sand creams the sea.
Trotting, trotting,
Not in a straight line,
But,
Zagging the cream-lined sea.
Trotting between its fore paws,
The dog,
Walks a crab into its hole
And,
Digging it out again,
Scampers with shock or glee.
The dog trots on,
On,
On the long unwinding beach
Then,
Sights a stump
A sun bleached stump
And,
Breaking off,
Hurries,
Circles and inspects,
And salutes.
The dog is trotting home
Trotting,
Trotting to its home
Trotting by the wine horizoned sea
Trotting
Trotting into the dusk
And home

Wilfred H. Taylor

14th

IF YOU SHOULD MEET A CROCODILE

If you should meet a crocodile,
Don't take a stick and poke him;
Ignore the welcome in his smile,
Be careful not to stroke him.
For he sleeps upon the Nile,
He thinner gets and thinner;
But whene'er you meet a crocodile
He's ready for his dinner.

Anonymous

15th

HIPPO WRITES A LOVE POEM TO HIS WIFE

Oh, my beautiful fat wife
Larger to me than life
Smile broader than the River Nile
My winsome waddlesome
You do me proud in the shallow of morning
You do me proud in the deep night
Oh, my bodysome mud-basking companion.

John Agard

16th

HOW DOTH...

How doth the little crocodile
  Improve his shining tail,
And pour the waters of the Nile
  On every golden scale!

How cheerfully he seems to grin,
  How neatly spreads his claws,
And welcomes little fishes in
  With gently smiling jaws!

Lewis Carroll

17th

GIRAFFE

How lucky
To live
So high
Above
The body,
Breathing
At heaven's
Level,
Looking
Sun
In the eye;
While down
Below
The neck's
Precarious
Stair,
Back, belly,
And legs
Take care
Of themselves,
Hardly
Aware
Of the head's
Airy
Affairs.

Valerie Worth

18th

THE GAZELLE CALF

The gazelle calf, O my children,
goes behind its mother across the desert,
goes behind its mother on blithe bare foot
requiring no shoes, O my children!

D. H. Lawrence

19th

SNAKE MOVING

With undulations
From side to side
Through tall grasses
with footless stride
I glide.

While my double tongue
Like twin sticks
Is feeling its way around
As it flicks
And licks.

Olive Dove

20th

A PUZZLED PYTHON

A puzzled python shook its head
and said, "I simply fail
to tell if I am purely neck,
or else entirely tail."

Jack Prelutsky

21st

MONKEY

Have you ever watched a monkey
Climbing up a tree?
He can reach the tip-most top-most
Before you count to three.
And those who try to catch him
Just haven't got a chance.
Off he goes like a man in space
A monkey grin on his monkey face,
Legs and tail all over the place
And lands on another branch.

A cow may moo and a bee may buzz
But none can jump like a monkey does!

Herbert Kretzmer

22nd

SWALLOWS

Quick they are
      and slick they are
and swooping through
      the air
as if they couldn't
      stop for joy—
and joy had tossed them
      there.
Loud they are
      and proud they are,
and curving
      as they call,
fly all the way
      from Africa
without a map
      at all.

Jean Kenward

23rd

THE FIRST SWALLOW
(EXTRACT)

The gorse is yellow on the heath;
  The banks with speed-well flowers are gay;
The oaks are budding, and beneath,
  The hawthorn soon will bear the wreath,
The silver wreath of May.

The welcomed guest of settled spring,
The swallow, too, is come at last.

Charlotte Smith

24th

THE PEACOCK'S EYE

Mark you how the peacock's eye
Winks away its ring of green,
Barter'd for an azure dye,
And the piece that's like a bean,
The pupil, plays its liquid jet
To win a look of violet.

Gerard Manley Hopkins

25th

ELEPHANT ETERNITY

Elephants walking under juicy-leaf trees
Walking with their children under juicy-leaf trees
Elephants elephants walking like time

Elephants bathing in the foam-floody river
Fountaining their children in the mothery river
Elephants elephants bathing like happiness

Strong and gentle elephants
Standing on the earth
Strong and gentle elephants
Like peace

Time is walking under elephant trees
Happiness is bathing in the elephant river
Strong gentle peace is shining
All over the elephant earth

Adrian Mitchell

26th

THE ELEPHANT

The elephant carries a great big trunk;
He never packs it with clothes;
It has no lock and it has no key,
But he takes it wherever he goes.

Anonymous

27th
WELCOMING THE BIRDS

You hold up your hand.

Now your hand's a tree.

Small birds fly to it

Gratefully

And they rest their wings,

Your sweet-singing friends,

As they perch like snowflakes

On your fingers' ends.

Adrian Mitchell

28th

WOODPECKER

Carving
tap/tap
music
out of
tap/tap
tree trunk
keep me
busy
whole day
tap/tap
long

tap/tap
pecker
birdsong
tap/tap
pecker
birdsong

tree bark
is tap/tap
drumskin
fo me beak
I keep
tap/tap
rhythm
fo forest
heartbeat

tap/tap
chisel beak
long
tap/tap
honey leak
song
pecker/tap
tapper/peck
pecker
birdsong

John Agard

29th

BIRD SIPS WATER

Bird
sips water
drips music
throwing back its head

throw back your head
turn the rain
into a song
and you will fly

Keith Bosley

30th

THE LEAPING HARE

Darts down the road,
Melts into grass, stock still,
Drums on the still moon,
Is hunted and, grey with age,
Leaps. And is gone.

George Szirtes

31st

ABOVE

A lone grey heron is flying, flying
         Home to her nest,
And over the rush-blown waters
         Burning in the west,
Where an orange moon is lying
         Softly on soft air,
As the dusk comes lounging after
         Sleepy care.

Ah, now that heron is slowly, slowly
         Plying her wing,
But soon she'll droop to the rushes
         Where the winds swing;
She'll stand in the pools and coldly
         Dream on the sly,
With her wild eyes watching the fishes,
         As stars watch you from on high.

F. R. Higgins

APRIL

1st

THE ALLIGATOR

The alligator chased his tail
Which hit him on the snout;
He nibbled, gobbled, swallowed it,
And turned right inside-out.

Mary Macdonald

2nd

MISSISSIPPI ALLIGATOR

Like a lumpy log on the limpid river,
floating near green forest bank,
pushing string-weed with a shiver,
where ferns drip heavy with the damp;
Mississippi alligator,
on the move again.

Summer rain makes water patterns,
turning, swinging water-wheels.
Round the houseboat's swaying lanterns
moths are dancing Irish reels;
Mississippi alligator,
on the move again.

Underneath the harvest moon,
rabbits' whiskers twitch and quiver.
Silent motion in the gloom,
breaks reflections on the river;
Mississippi alligator,
on the move again.

Robin Mellor

3rd

LAUGHTER'S FAVOURITE ANIMAL

I agree
rabbit is sweet
and chimpanzee
is very clever,
and you'll never beat
elephant for memory.

If you see
fierce tiger
you'd wish
you could run like ostrich,
or better yet had the feet
of cheetah.

Sure, parrot could chatter,
snake could change skin,
and for a pet
some would pick hamster.
For creepy-crawly feet
you might place a bet
on spider to win.

But alligator
has that special something.
Teeth that seem to laugh.
Teeth that seem to grin.

John Agard

4th

EASTER

The air is like a butterfly
    With frail blue wings.
The happy earth looks at the sky
    And sings.

Joyce Kilmer

5th

SPRING SONG

On the grassy banks
Lambkins at their pranks;
Woolly sisters, woolly brothers,
    Jumping off their feet,
While their woolly mothers
    Watch by them and bleat.

Christina Rossetti

6th

BABY CHICK

Peck
    peck
        peck
on the warm brown egg.
OUT comes a neck.
OUT comes a leg.

How
    does
        a chick
who's not been about,
discover the trick
of how to get out?

Aileen Fisher

8th

Paddling, we saw that turtle; saw its eyes open,
    its flippers outstretched, as it floated.
Seawater lapped at its shell, spreading across its back.

Rirratjiŋu clan song cycle,
Wandjuk Marika (attributed),
translated by Ronald Berndt

7th

JELLYFISH

When my chandelier
Waltzes pulsing near
Let the swimmer fear.

Beached and bare
I'm less of a scare.
But I don't care.

Though I look like a slob
It's a delicate job
Being just a blob.

Ted Hughes

9th

IF THE OCTOPUS . . .

If the octopus suddenly feels a wish
To dine on a plump young passing fish
He stays very still and he keeps very calm
And he reaches out arm after arm after arm.

A. S. J. Tessimond

10th

THE OCTOPUS

Tell me, O Octopus, I begs,
Is those things arms or is they legs?
I marvel at thee, Octopus;
If I were thou, I'd call me Us.

Ogden Nash

11th

SEAHORSE

O under the ocean waves
I gallop the seaweed lanes,
I jump the coral reef,
And all with no saddle or reins.

I haven't a flowing mane,
I've only this horsey face,
But under the ocean waves
I'm king of the steeplechase.

Blake Morrison

12th

FIREFOX

Fox fox
coat of fire
bush of flame
setting light
to April woods
firework trail
of powder, fuse
that sets aglow
with green and gold
the willow wands
the meadow grass
the pasture ponds
the primrose banks.

Fox fox fox
from winter runs
with torch for tail
and touches spring
to hill and copse
his foxfire fingers
flaming hedges
spreading shoots of
shivering blossom
in the sun—the ghost
of summertime
that trots beside
his crimson shadow's
violet and bluebell glades—

mysterious barks—fox, fox,
fox, fox-fox, fox, fox-fox-fox!

James Kirkup

13th

in a shimmer of air
the fox cubs are allowed to play
while the parent looks on

Nozawa Bonchō,
translated by Earl Miner and Hiroko Odagari

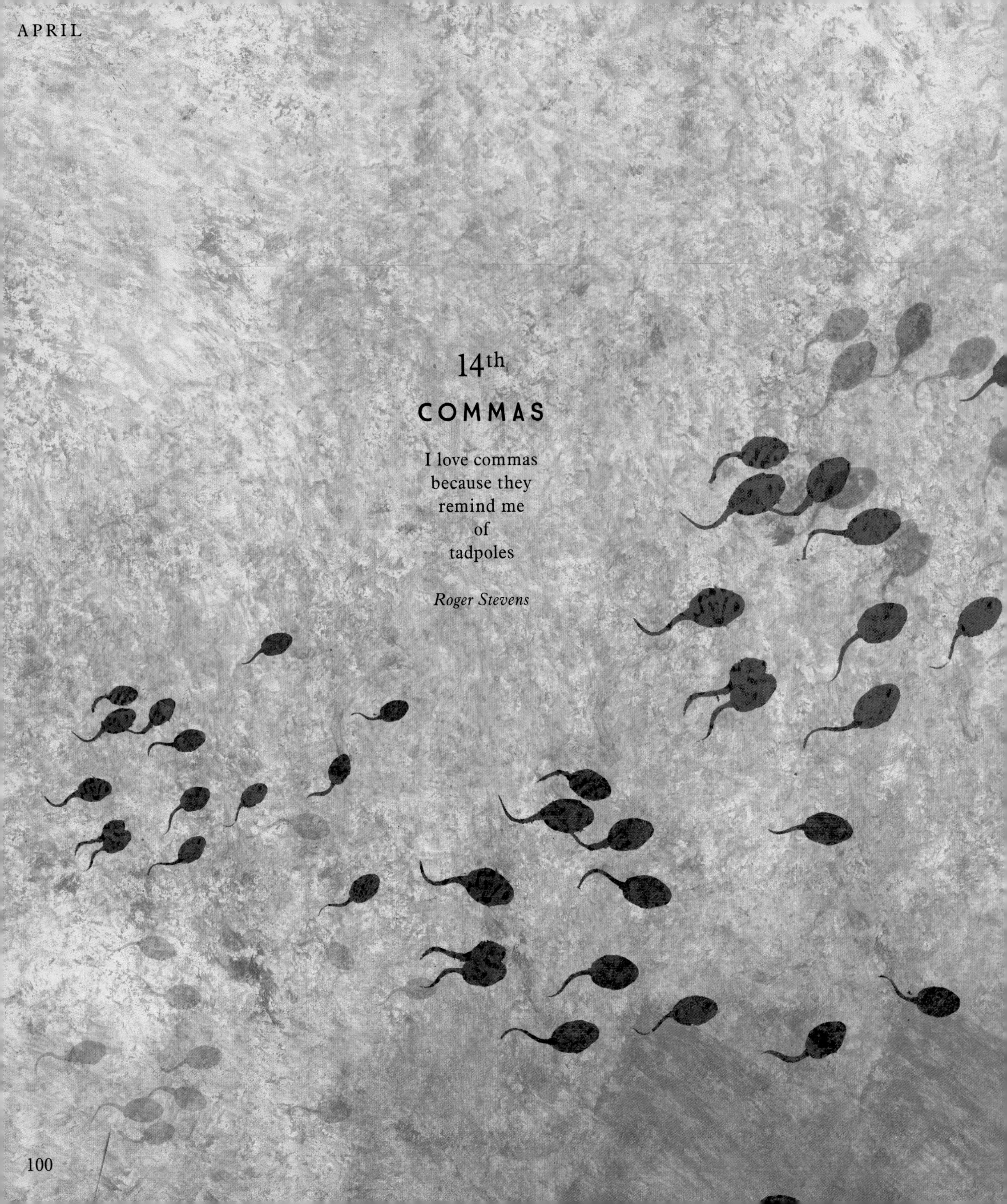

14th

COMMAS

I love commas
because they
remind me
of
tadpoles

Roger Stevens

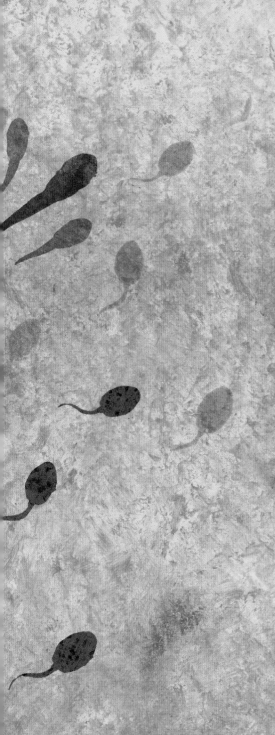

15th

MIRACLE

In June after a brief shower,
an astounding appearance of little green frogs,
as if a miracle had happened,
and they had fallen down from heaven.

In March they choked the pools and ditches,
and then masses of black-centred jelly eggs
floating with moorhens and tiny water-boatmen,
speckled trout rising.

April, legions of darting tadpoles,
needle tails and bullet heads growing,
until, one evening, the cycle almost over,
first frogs leaping out
to cover the land like a plague.

The frenzied croaking died down,
they move solitary into damp garden corners,
under stones, on to reedy river banks,
juicy prey for sharp-eyed heron.

Next year, the same miracle.

Leonard Clark

16th

THE MAGNIFICENT BULL

My bull is white like the silver fish in the river,
White like the shimmering crane bird on the river bank
White like fresh milk!
His roar is like thunder to the Turkish cannon
      on the steep shore.
My bull is dark like the raincloud in the storm.
He is like summer and winter.
Half of him is dark like the storm cloud
Half of him is light like sunshine.
His back shines like the morning star.
His brow is red like the back of the hornbill.
His forehead is like a flag, calling the people from
      a distance.
He resembles the rainbow.

I will water him at the river,
With my spear I shall drive my enemies.
Let them water their herds at the well;
The river belongs to me and my bull.
Drink, my bull, from the river; I am here
to guard you with my spear.

Dinka poem,
translator unknown

17th

WILD BLACK CROWS

Oh the wild black crows
The wild black crows
Fly far away to where nobody knows,
Where nobody knows and nobody goes,
Nobody knows
But the wild black crows.

Margaret Wise Brown

18th

PRAYER FOR EARTH

Last night
an owl
called from the hill.
Coyotes howled.
A deer stood still
nibbling at bushes far away.
The moon shone silver.
Let this stay.

Today
two noisy crows
flew by,
their shadows pasted on the sky.
The sun broke out
through clouds of gray.
An iris opened.
Let this stay.

Myra Cohn Livingston

19th

The morning is leaking out
The coyote wolf
Is calling, is calling

Southern Paiute song,
translated by John Wesley Powell

20th

The long night;
The monkey thinks how
To catch hold of the moon.

Masaoka Shiki,
translated by R. H. Blyth

21st

THE ANIMAL FAIR

We went to the Animal Fair,
The birds and the beasts were there.
The big baboon by the light of the moon
Was combing his auburn hair.

The monkey fell out of his bunk
Right on to the elephant's trunk,
The elephant sneezed and fell on his knees
And what became of the monkey,
Monkey, monkey, monkey, monk?

Anonymous

22nd

GORILLAS

Moonlight upon the mountains
And the gentle Gorillas awake

They lumber along through the forest
To sit by the side of the lake

And there in the silvery water
They dangle their ticklish toes

And what the Gorillas are thinking
Nobody nobody knows

Adrian Mitchell

23th

THE CODFISH

The codfish lays ten thousand eggs,
    The homely hen lays one.
The codfish never cackles
    To tell you what she's done.
And so we scorn the codfish,
    While the humble hen we prize,
Which only goes to show you
    That it pays to advertise.

Anonymous

24th

FISH

Look at them flit
Lickety-split
Wiggling
Swiggling
Swerving
Curving
Hurrying
Scurrying
Chasing
Racing
Whizzing
Whisking
Flying
Frisking
Tearing around
With a leap and a bound
But none of them making the tiniest
tiniest
tiniest
sound.

Mary Ann Hoberman

25th

ANSWER TO A CHILD'S QUESTION

Do you ask what the birds say? The Sparrow, the Dove,
The Linnet and Thrush say, "I love and I love!"
In the winter they're silent—the wind is so strong;
What it says, I don't know, but it sings a loud song.
But green leaves, and blossoms, and sunny warm weather,
And singing, and loving—all come back together.
But the Lark is so brimful of gladness and love,
The green fields below him, the blue sky above,
That he sings, and he sings; and for ever sings he—
"I love my Love, and my Love loves me!"

Samuel Taylor Coleridge

26th

All the long day—
Yet not long enough for the skylark,
Singing, singing.

Matsuo Bashō,
translated by R. H. Blyth

27th

RABBIT AND LARK

"Under the ground
        It's rumbly and dark
And interesting,"
        Said Rabbit to Lark.

Said Lark to Rabbit,
        "Up in the sky
There's plenty of room
        And it's airy and high."

"Under the ground
        It's warm and dry.
Won't you live with me?"
        Was Rabbit's reply.

"The air's so sunny.
        I wish you'd agree,"
Said the little Lark,
        "To live with me."

But under the ground
        And up in the sky,
Larks can't burrow
        Nor rabbits fly.

So Skylark over
        And Rabbit under
They had to settle
        To live asunder.

And often these two friends
        Meet with a will
For a chat together
        On top of the hill.

James Reeves

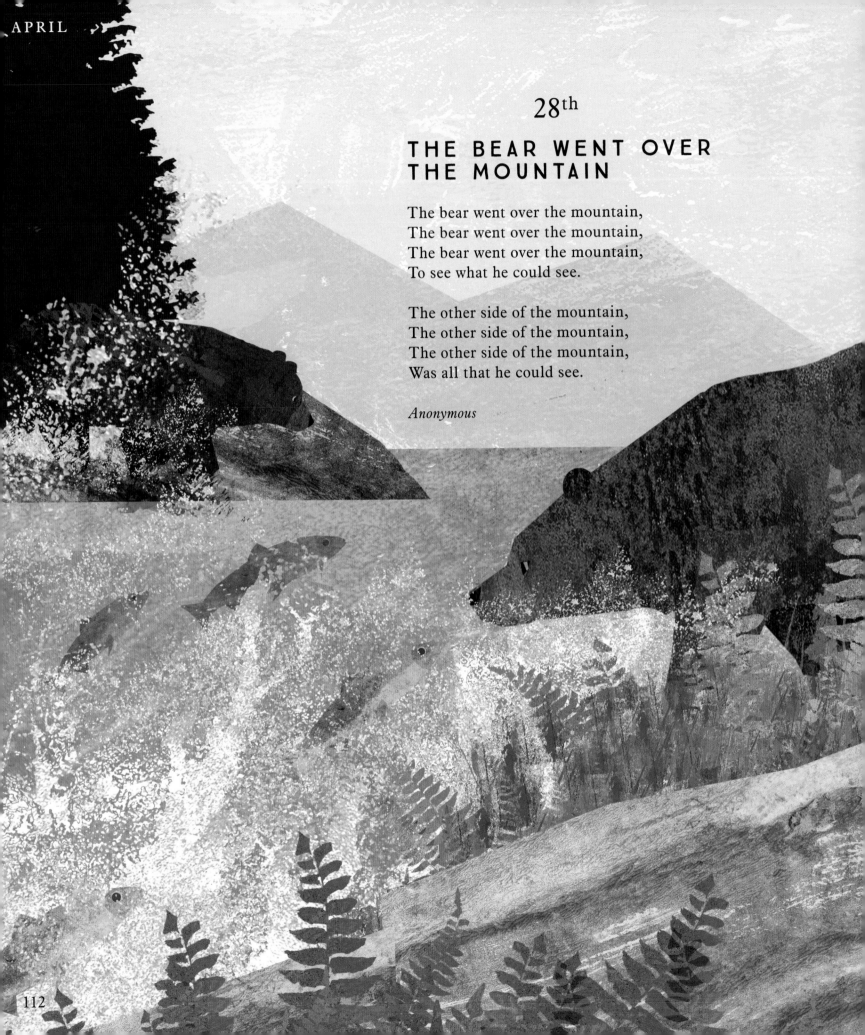

28th

THE BEAR WENT OVER THE MOUNTAIN

The bear went over the mountain,
The bear went over the mountain,
The bear went over the mountain,
To see what he could see.

The other side of the mountain,
The other side of the mountain,
The other side of the mountain,
Was all that he could see.

Anonymous

29th

HERE COME THE BEARS

Clambering through the rocky torrents
Here come the bears
Quicksilver salmon flip into the light
to flop a little higher up
swerving past scooping claws
and underwater gaping muzzles
to flip up into the light again
past the black tip
of the nose of a small bear
his eyes as wide as all amazement

Adrian Mitchell

30th

THE SMALL BROWN BEAR

The small brown bear
fishes
with stony paws

eating ice salmon
all waterfall slippery
till his teeth ache.

Michael Baldwin

MAY

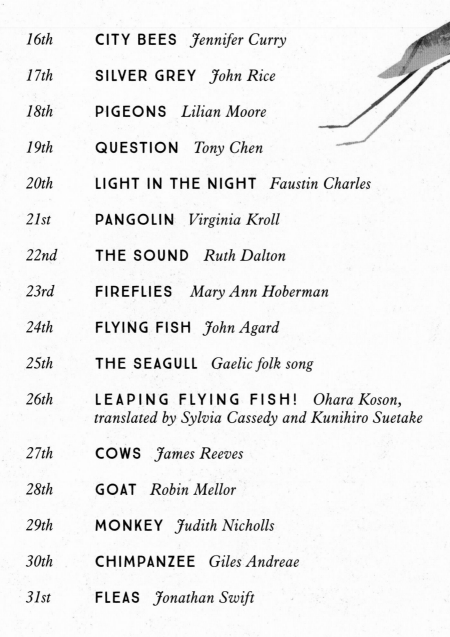

1st

SONG ABOUT THE REINDEER, MUSK OXEN, WOMEN, AND MEN WHO WANT TO SHOW OFF (EXTRACT)

It's wonderful to see
the reindeer come down
from the forest,
and start pouring north
over the white tundra,
anxiously avoiding pit-falls in the snow.
        Jai-ja-jija.

Inuit song,
translated by Tom Lowenstein

2nd

I hear everything,
I hear everything.
I am the crow,
I am the crow.

Arapaho song,
translated by James Mooney

4th
BAT WORDS

Why do people
get tightup,
because we here
hang downside up?

Are scared they of
our bat wings black?
Or of our knees
on front to back?

We're bottom up,
but don't please fuss—
for you're the way
round wrong to us!

Liz Brownlee

3rd
ROOKERY

Here they come, freckling the sunset,
The slow big sailers bearing down
On the plantation. They have flown
Their sorties and are now well met.

The upper twigs dip and wobble
With each almost two-point landing,
Then ride to rest. There is nothing
Else to do now only settle.

But they keep up a guttural chat
As stragglers knock the roost see-saw.
Something's satisfied in that caw.
Who wouldn't come to rest like that?

Seamus Heaney

5th

THE KINGFISHER

When Noah left the Ark, the animals
Capered and gambolled on the squadgy soil,
Enjoying their new-found freedom; and the birds
Soared upwards, twittering, to the open skies.
But one soared higher than the rest, in utter ecstasy,
Till all his back and wings were drenched
With the vivid blue of heaven itself, and his breast
      scorched
With the upward-slanting rays of the setting sun.
When he came back to earth, he had lost the Ark;
His friends were all dispersed. So now he soars no more;
A lonely bird, he darts and dives for fish,
By streams and pools—places where water is—
Still searching, but in vain, for the vanished Ark
And rain-washed terraces of Ararat.

John Heath-Stubbs

6th

the kingfisher;
on its wet feathers
shines the evening sun

Tōri,
translated by R. H. Blyth

7th

OTTER

I knew the river hid
behind the bank,
lying, like a length of silk,
stretched between the willows.

The surface ripped,
something dived—
gone too long to be a bird.

Eager head above the water,
down he went again,
a flash of oily fur.

He swam up beside,
this time he stayed,
looking at me straight.
I walked to keep his pace.

I loved his length—
his tail his body,
his body his tail,
his tail the river's length.

We moved together
through the wind,
along the river's course.

Another dive,
I skimmed the current,
searching for his guise.

He'd gone on alone.
I felt him though,
gliding through
the river's strength.

Chrissie Gittins

8th

MOLE

velvet coat
sharp teeth
spade hand
digs beneath

soil sprays
black fountains
high hills
small mountains

pink snout
seeks worms
bites wriggles
eats squirms

Jan Dean

9th

THE WORM

When the earth is turned in spring
The worms are fat as anything.

And birds come flying all around
To eat the worms right off the ground.

They like worms just as much as I
Like bread and milk and apple pie.

And once, when I was very young,
I put a worm right on my tongue.

I didn't like the taste a bit,
And so I didn't swallow it.

But oh, it makes my mother squirm
Because she *thinks* I ate that worm!

Ralph Bergengren

10th

LEAF-EATER

On a shrub in the heart of the garden,
On an outer leaf, a grub twists
Half its body, a tendril,
This way and that in blind
Space, no leaf or twig
Anywhere in reach; then gropes
Back on itself and begins
To eat its own leaf.

Thomas Kinsella

11th

MINIBEAST MOVEMENTS

This is the way the beetle stumbles,
clumsy, clockwork, slow.

This is the way the grasshopper leaps,
so! so! so!

This is the way the snail slides,
smooth, steady, sure.

And this is the way the spider scuttles,
swiftly across the floor!

Tony Mitton

12th

ZEBRA

Who let them loose
with face paints?
Who gave them pyjamas
to wear?
Who made them look
like newspapers?
Who striped them
here and there?

Who designed them
like mint humbugs?
Who painted them
white and black?
Who thought of
a different pattern
for each new
zebra's back?

Moira Andrew

13th

THE OSTRICH

The ostrich roams the great Sahara.
Its mouth is wide, its neck is narra.
It has such long and lofty legs,
I'm glad it sits to lay its eggs.

Ogden Nash

14th

RHINOCEROS

God simply got bored and started doodling
with ideas he'd given up on, scooping off the floor
bits and bobs and sticking them together:
the tail of a ten-ton pig he'd meant for Norway,
the long skull of a top-heavy dinosaur,
the armour-plating of his first version of
the hippo, an unpainted beak of a toucan
stuck on back to front, a dash of tantrums
he'd intended for the Abyssinian owl, the same
awful grey colour he used for landscaping the moon.

And tempted to try it with the batteries,
he set it down on the wild plains of Africa,
grinned at what he saw and let it run.

Matt Simpson

15th

A MEMORY OF KENYA

The neck of an ostrich makes a J;
And though its kneejoints bend the wrong way
It travels at almost the speed of sound,
Its head and body parallel to the ground;
And its droppings are silver waterfalls
On the hot dry plains of Africa.

Roy Fuller

16th
CITY BEES

In a drab back yard
At the back of his shop
Among boxes and bins
A world away
From flowering fields
And hedgerows in blossom
Mr Patel keeps bees.

City bees.
They browse on buddleia and
Ragged weeds
Rosebay willowherb
And dust-heavy trees
But their busy wings
Bring sweetness
To the city.

Jennifer Curry

17th
SILVER GREY

a silver grey ripple
on
a grey silver river:
the squirrel crosses the road

John Rice

18th

PIGEONS

Pigeons are city folk
content
to live with concrete
and cement.

They seldom
try
the sky.

A pigeon never sings
of hill
and flowering hedge,
but busily commutes
from sidewalk
to his ledge.
      Oh pigeon, what a waste of wings!

Lilian Moore

19th

QUESTION

As asphalt and concrete
Replace bushes and trees,
As highways and buildings
Replace marshes and woods,
What will replace
The song of the birds?

Tony Chen

20th

LIGHT IN THE NIGHT

Fireflies trail through the dark
And a spark
Lights every candle in the night.
Nearer than stars
They brighten night-time smiles.
Dancing little flames
They flicker their names
Around for miles
Shining through eyes of the moon.
On wings of their light
The night takes flight
And disappears in glittering skies.

Faustin Charles

21st

PANGOLIN

Pangolin, pangolin,
        unfurl for me,
Curled in a branch at
        the top of our tree.
With scales in layers,
        you hang in your home,
Looking to all like a
        giant pine cone.

Virginia Kroll

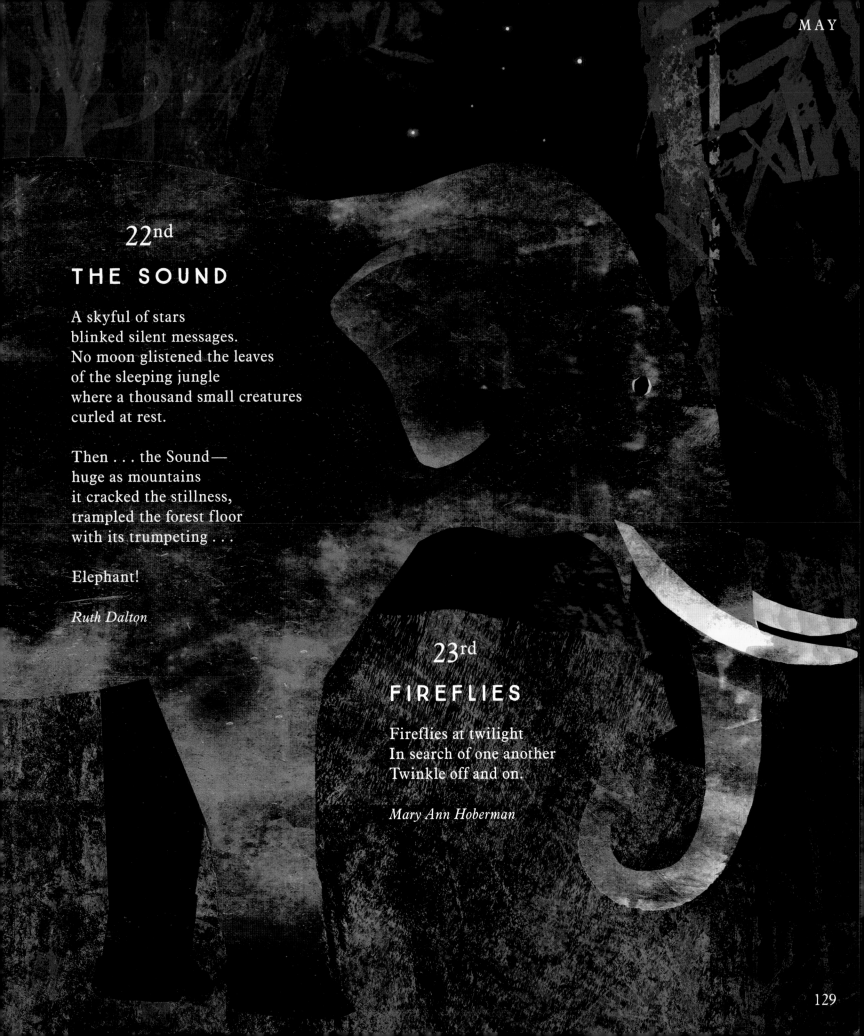

22nd

THE SOUND

A skyful of stars
blinked silent messages.
No moon glistened the leaves
of the sleeping jungle
where a thousand small creatures
curled at rest.

Then . . . the Sound—
huge as mountains
it cracked the stillness,
trampled the forest floor
with its trumpeting . . .

Elephant!

Ruth Dalton

23rd

FIREFLIES

Fireflies at twilight
In search of one another
Twinkle off and on.

Mary Ann Hoberman

24th

FLYING FISH

Flying fish
flying fish
what is your wish?

In water
you swim
yet like to skim
through wind

Flying fish
flying fish
make up your mind

Are you a bird
inside a fish
or just a fish
dreaming of wings?

John Agard

25th

THE SEAGULL

All day long o'er the ocean I fly,
My white wings beating fast through the sky,
I hunt fishes all down the bay
And ride on rocking billows in play.

All night long in my rock home I rest,
Away up on a cliff is my nest,
The waves murmur, murmur below,
And winds fresh from the sea o'er me blow.

Gaelic folk song

26th

Leaping flying fish!
Dancing for me and my boat
as I sail for home.

*Ohara Koson,
translated by Sylvia Cassedy and Kunihiro Suetake*

27th

COWS

Half the time they munched the grass, and all the time they lay
Down in the water-meadows, the lazy month of May,
A-chewing,
A-mooing,
To pass the hours away.

"Nice weather," said the brown cow.
"Ah," said the white.
"Grass is very tasty."
"Grass is all right."

Half the time they munched the grass, and all the time they lay
Down in the water-meadows, the lazy month of May,
A-chewing,
A-mooing,
To pass the hours away.

"Rain coming," said the brown cow.
"Ah," said the white.
"Flies is very tiresome."
"Flies bite."

Half the time they munched the grass, and all the time they lay
Down in the water-meadows, the lazy month of May,
A-chewing,
A-mooing,
To pass the hours away.

"Time to go," said the brown cow.
"Ah," said the white.
"Nice chat." "Very pleasant."
"Night." "Night."

Half the time they munched the grass, and all the time they lay
Down in the water-meadows, the lazy month of May,
A-chewing,
A-mooing,
To pass the hours away.

James Reeves

28th

GOAT

He chews the fresh grass
and remembers . . .

the taste of red-spotted handkerchiefs
and a new pair of tights,
in the days before his half-moon
horns grew to rough white.

His eyes glisten like marbles,
when he thinks of the fun
he had rushing round the farmyard,
with the farmer's young son.

A grown goat must be sensible,
and quiet and wise,
but, though he's out in the field now,
the gleam is still in his eyes.

He chews the fresh grass
and remembers . . .

Robin Mellor

29th

MONKEY

I am
swing-on-a-tail,
up with the sun
fast as white lightning
slits skies at noon.
Now under palms,
now over fern;
dawn-creeper, branch-leaper,
dive, twist and turn.
Face-in-the-forest,
chasing the moon;
tree-lover, sky-brother,
dew-dancing one.

Judith Nicholls

30th

CHIMPANZEE

It's great to be a chimpanzee
Swinging through the trees
And if we can't find nuts to eat
We munch each other's fleas!

Giles Andreae

31st

FLEAS

So, Nat'ralists observe, a Flea
Hath smaller fleas that on him prey,
And these have smaller Fleas to bite 'em,
And so proceed *ad infinitum*.

Jonathan Swift

JUNE

16th   **EAGLE**   *Papago song,*
translated by Ruth Murray Underhill

17th   **HARES AT PLAY**   *John Clare*

18th   **HARE**   *Adele Davide*

19th   **ROLL PLAY**   *Sandy Brownjohn*

20th   **SNAKE**   *Angela Topping*

21st   **YOU SPOTTED SNAKES WITH DOUBLE TONGUE**
William Shakespeare, A Midsummer Night's Dream

22nd   **HEDGEHOG HUGS**   *Liz Brownlee*

23rd   **THE HUMMINGBIRD**   *Michael Flanders*

24th   **BEE**   *X. J. Kennedy*

25th   **HUMMINGBIRDS AND BEES**   *Pauline Stewart*

26th   **BEES CANNOT FLY**   *Roger McGough*

27th   **THE PARADOXICAL LEOPARD**   *Colin West*

28th   **THE HYENA**   *Mike Thaler*

29th   **CAREFUL!**   *Anonymous*

30th   **AN ELEPHANT IS BORN**   *Liz Brownlee*

1st

LARK

You'll hear me before you see me,
spilling notes from high skies,
I don't pause for breath—
my song, without doubt, is the best.

You might see me as a speck in the clouds,
I'll grow bigger, disappear altogether,
but still I'm thrilling the heavens,
hanging over the land.

I dare any other lark to come near,
I'll thrash him out of my patch
filling the atmosphere with
my thirty-six notes a minute.

I'm second to none,
dive-bombing back through the sky
to keep a fair eye on my mate
as she waits in the grass.

We have wide-mouthed babies to make.

Chrissie Gittins

2nd

SUMMER
(EXTRACT)

Winter is cold-hearted
    Spring is yea and nay,
Autumn is a weathercock
    Blown every way:
Summer days for me
When every leaf is on its tree;

When Robin's not a beggar,
    And Jenny Wren's a bride,
And larks hang singing, singing, singing,
    Over the wheatfields wide,
    And anchored lilies ride,
And the pendulum spider
    Swings from side to side.

Christina Rossetti

3rd

A RACKETEERING CROWD

June night, two points shine
claws skitter down waving tail
ratcheting sounds of possums

Joe Maverick

4th

THE GOLDEN BIRD

I watched the new moon fly
behind a summit tree
to perch on an upper branch
and so look down at me.

Upon that very instant,
the glowing gully rang
with a kookaburra's laughter,
while frogs and crickets sang.

I was a dreamy lad,
walking the bush alone:
it was thirty years ago . . .
In all that I have known,

the frogs have never croaked,
the crickets never chirred,
so blithely as on that night
when the moon was a laughing bird,

new moon, a golden bird,
perched high, with beak in air,
when I was a dreamy lad
and the bush was everywhere.

Rex Ingamells

5th

THE WATER VOLE

He lives beneath the sally-hedge,
Beside the placid water's edge,
Within a bunch of foxes-sedge,
Growing on a moss-sprinkled ridge.

At close of day when he awakes,
He listens to the brown corncrakes,
The bullfrogs in the rushy brakes,
And dives and swims in nearby lakes.

D. J. O'Sullivan

6th

LITTLE FROG

Little frog among
rain-shaken leaves, are you, too,
splashed with green paint?

Gaki,
translator unknown

7th

TODAY I SAW THE DRAGONFLY

Today I saw the dragonfly
Come from the wells where he did lie.

An inner impulse rent the veil
Of his old husk: from head to tail
Came out clear plates of sapphire mail.

He dried his wings: like gauze they grew;
Through crofts and pastures wet with dew
A living flash of light, he flew.

Alfred, Lord Tennyson

8th

GRASSHOPPERS

Grasshoppers go in many a thrumming spring
And now to stalks of tasselled sour-grass cling,
That shakes and sways awhile, but still keeps straight
While arching oxeye doubles with his weight.
Next on the cat-tail grass with farther bound
He springs, that bends until they touch the ground.

John Clare

9th

LADYBUG

A small speckled visitor
    wearing crimson cape,
brighter than a cherry,
    smaller than a grape.

A polka-dotted someone
    walking on my wall,
a black-hooded lady
    in a scarlet shawl.

Joan Walsh Anglund

10th

PRAYER OF THE BUTTERFLY

Lord!
Where was I?
Oh yes! This flower, this sun,
Thank You! Your world is beautiful!
This scent of roses . . .
Where was I?
A drop of dew
Rolls to sparkle in a lily's heart.
I have to go . . .
Where? I do not know!

Carmen Bernos de Gasztold,
translated by Rumer Godden

11th

GREEN STEMS

Little things that crawl and creep
In the green grass forests,
Deep in their long-stemmed world
Where ferns uncurl
To a greener world
Beneath the leaves above them;
And every flower upon its stem
Blows above them there
The bottom of a geranium,
The back side of a trillium,
The belly of a bumblebee
Is all they see, these little things
Down so low
Where no bird sings
Where no winds blow,
Deep in their long-stemmed world.

Margaret Wise Brown

12th

RACCOON

One summer night a little Raccoon,
Above his left shoulder, looked at the new moon.
    He made a wish;
    He said: "I wish
    I were a Catfish,
    A Blowfish, a Squid,
    A Katydid,
    A Beetle, a Skink,
    An Ostrich, a pink
    Flamingo, a Gander,
    A Salamander,
    A Hippopotamus,
    A Duck-billed Platypus,
    A Gecko, a Slug,
    A Water Bug,
    A pug-nosed Beaver,
    Anything whatever
Except what I am, a little Raccoon!"

Above his left shoulder, the Evening Star
Listened and heard the little Raccoon
    Who wished on the moon;
    And she said: "Why wish
    You were a Catfish,
    A Blowfish, a Squid,
    A Katydid,
    A Beetle, a Skink,
    An Ostrich, a pink
    Flamingo, a Gander,
    A Salamander,
    A Hippopotamus,
    A Duck-billed Platypus,
    A Gecko, a Slug,
    A Water Bug,
    A pug-nosed Beaver,
    Anything whatever?
Why must you change?" said the Evening Star.
"When you are perfect as you are?
I know a boy who wished on the moon
That *he* might be a little Raccoon."

William Jay Smith

13th

Foxes playing
Among the narcissus flowers—
A bright moonlit night.

Yosa Buson,
translated by R. H. Blyth

14th

GRIZZLY BEAR

If you ever, ever, ever
    meet a grizzly bear,
You must never, never, never
    ask him where
He is going,
Or *what* he is doing;
For if you ever, ever dare
To stop a grizzly bear,
You will never
Meet *another* grizzly bear.

Mary Austin

15th

The blue water in
The Mountain cañon
The grizzly bear on the mountain
Is digging

Southern Paiute song,
translated by John Wesley Powell

16th

EAGLE

The sun's rays
Lie along my wings
And stretch beyond their tips.

Papago song,
translated by Ruth Murray Underhill

17th

HARES AT PLAY

The birds are gone to bed, the cows are still,
And sheep lie panting on each old mole-hill;
And underneath the willow's grey-green bough,
Like a toil a-resting, lies the fallow plough.
The timid hares throw daylight fears away
On the lane's road to dust and dance and play,
Then dabble in the grain by naught deterred
To lick the dew-fall from the barley's beard;
Then out they start again and round the hill
Like happy thoughts dance, squat, and loiter still,
Till milking maidens in the early morn
Jingle their yokes and start them in the corn;
Through well-known beaten paths each nimbling hare
Starts quick as fear, and seeks its hidden lair.

John Clare

18th

HARE

Midsummer madness
And the March hare
Galloping across fields
With nowhere to go but home
And happy for it.

Adele Davide

19th

ROLL PLAY

Two stoats chasing down a country lane
Threading over and under each other;
Chestnut fur in a twisted skein,
Flashes of white as they blend together,
Black-tip tails woven into the grain,
Twined in one continuous slither—
A moment of summer that will remain.

Sandy Brownjohn

20th

SNAKE

Snake
Tessellated
Oiled smoother
Sliding S
Shapes along
Wiggly tickly
Warm to the touch
Pointy-tongued
Clever old
Snake.

Angela Topping

21st

You spotted snakes with double tongue,
Thorny hedgehogs, be not seen;
Newts and blindworms, do no wrong,
Come not near our Fairy Queen.

Philomele, with melody
Sing in our sweet lullaby;
Lulla, lulla, lullaby, lulla, lulla, lullaby:
Never harm
Nor spell nor charm,
Come our lovely lady nigh;
So, good night, with lullaby.

Weaving spiders, come not here;
Hence, you long-legged spinners, hence!
Beetles black, approach not near;
Worm nor snail, do no offence.

Philomele, with melody
Sing in our sweet lullaby;
Lulla, lulla, lullaby, lulla, lulla, lullaby:
Never harm
Nor spell nor charm,
Come our lovely lady nigh;
So, good night, with lullaby.

William Shakespeare,
A Midsummer Night's Dream

22nd

HEDGEHOG HUGS

A hedgehog's hug is mainly hid
beneath its sharp and spiky lid,
and when it rolls into a ball
a hedgehog has no hug at all.

Liz Brownlee

23rd

THE HUMMINGBIRD

The Hummingbird, he has no song
From flower to flower he hums along
Humming his way among the trees
He finds no words for what he sees

Michael Flanders

24th

BEE

You want to make some honey?
All right. Here's the recipe.
Pour the juice of a thousand flowers
Through the sweet tooth of a Bee.

X. J. Kennedy

26th

BEES CANNOT FLY

Bees cannot fly, scientists have proved it.
It is all to do with wingspan and body weight.
Aerodynamically incapable of sustained flight
Bees simply cannot fly. And yet they do.

There's one there, unaware of its dodgy ratios,
A noisy bubble, a helium-filled steamroller.
Fat and proud of it, buzzing around the garden
As if it were the last day of the spring sales.

Trying on all the brightest flowers, squeezing itself
Into frilly numbers three sizes too small.
Bees can fly, there's no need to prove it. And sting.
When stung, do scientists refuse to believe it?

Roger McGough

25th

HUMMINGBIRDS AND BEES

Hummingbirds and bees both like pollen
and another thing they have in common
is humming all the words they have forgotten.

Pauline Stewart

27th

THE PARADOXICAL LEOPARD

The spots the leopard's
Been allotted
Are there so leopards
Can't be spotted.

Colin West

28th

THE HYENA

The hyena is
A funny bloke,
He'll laugh at almost
Any joke,
So if you have
A joke that's dim,
Go and tell your joke
To him.

Mike Thaler

29th

CAREFUL!

pull
a
rope
and
the
rope
pulls
in
the
forest
and
with
the
forest
leopards
come
to
town.

Anonymous

157

30th

AN ELEPHANT IS BORN

Night holds them safe,
the cloud moon gleams,
deep in the darkness
of soft breath and dreams,

the elephant mother
greets her new son,
with a tender and gentle,
low, soft hum,

strokes his face
the night-left long,
and sings her newborn
elephant song.

Liz Brownlee

JULY

1st

A NARROW FELLOW
IN THE GRASS

A narrow fellow in the grass
Occasionally rides;
You may have met him,—did you not?
His notice sudden is.

The grass divides as with a comb,
A spotted shaft is seen;
And then it closes at your feet
And opens further on.

He likes a boggy acre,
A floor too cool for corn.
Yet when a boy, and barefoot,
I more than once, at noon,

Have passed, I thought, a whip-lash
Unbraiding in the sun,—
When, stooping to secure it,
It wrinkled, and was gone.

Several of nature's people
I know, and they know me;
I feel for them a transport
Of cordiality;

But never met this fellow,
Attended or alone,
Without a tighter breathing,
And zero at the bone.

Emily Dickinson

2nd

WHO AM I?
(A KENNING)

Stripy pullover
Sharp stinger
Buzzing buzzer
Honey bringer

Paul Cookson

3rd

THE TŪĪ

The tūī is a chortle bird
a chatter bird, a chitter bird, a chuttle bird.

She wears her feather bow
her snowy bow, her foamy bow, her white bow,

on her shining black
her sheeny black, her coal black, her blue black,

in the skinny tree
the spindly tree, the spandly tree, the cabbage tree,

with her gargle song
her giggle song, her glaggle song, her tūī song.

Paula Green

4th

SNAKE

The word begins to
hiss as soon as the first
letter
goes on   S
s-s-s-s-s-s   forked tongue flickers
Hard eyes stare

Already the rest of the poem
shrinks back from
his narrow speed   The paper
draws in its breath   S N A K E
loops around the pencil
slides
among typewriter keys   slips
like a silk shoelace
away

Barbara Esbensen

5th

MONGOOSE

Mongoose mongoose
You can frighten snakes
Mongoose—strongoose
Think of the courage it takes.

Spike Milligan

6th

THE SCORPION

The Scorpion is as black as soot,
He dearly loves to bite;
He is a most unpleasant brute
To find in bed at night.

Hilaire Belloc

7th

THE MEERKATS OF AFRICA

Meerkats go about in packs,
They don't hang loose—
They're not really *cats* at all,
But more a mongoose.
They have great capabilities,
Make no mistake,
A Meerkat can kill a scorpion
Or even a snake.
They rescue each other's children
And have lookouts when they're feeding
And a system of babysitters—
The kind of co-operation
That the human race is needing!

Gavin Ewart

8th

UPON A SNAIL
(EXTRACT)

She goes but softly, but she goeth sure;
      She stumbles not, as stronger creatures do;
Her journey's shorter, so she may endure
      Better than they which do much further go.

She makes no noise, but stilly seizeth on
      The flower or herb appointed for her food;
The which she quietly doth feed upon,
      While others range and glare, but find no good.

And though she doth but very softly go,
      However slow her pace be, yet tis sure:
And certainly they that do travel so
      The prize which they do aim at they procure.

John Bunyan

9th

      Where can he be going
In the rain
      This snail?

Kobayashi Issa,
translated by R. H. Blyth

10th

SNAIL

Snail upon the wall,
Have you got at all
Anything to tell
About your shell?

Only this, my child—
When the wind is wild,
Or when the sun is hot,
It's all I've got.

John Drinkwater

11th

THE LION

stands alone
on the grassy plain.

He has his pride;
he shakes his mane.

In his eye
the sunset glistens:

when he roars,
the wide world listens.

David Elliott

12th

THE MUSICAL LION

Said the Lion: "On music I dote,
But something is wrong with my throat.
When I practise a scale,
The listeners quail,
And flee at the very first note!"

Oliver Herford

13th

LION

The lion, ruler over all the beasts,
Triumphant moves upon the grassy plain
With sun like gold upon his tawny brow
And dew like silver on his shaggy mane.

Into himself he draws the rolling thunder,
Beneath his flinty paw great boulders quake;
He will dispatch the mouse to burrow under,
The little deer to shiver in the brake.

He sets the fierce whip of each serpent lashing,
The tall giraffe brings humbly to his knees,
Awakes the sloth, and sends the wild boar crashing,
Wide-eyed monkeys chittering, through the trees.

He gazes down into the quiet river,
Parting the green bulrushes to behold
A sunflower-crown of amethyst and silver,
A royal coat of brushed and beaten gold.

William Jay Smith

14th

KINGFISHER

Dropping
Like a splinter from the sky
It knives the water,
Swiftly strikes,
Turns, surges
Up through the splattering surface,
Back to the willow branch,
Where it sits triumphant,
Wet feathers glistening,
Its silver catch
Dangling from its beak.

John Foster

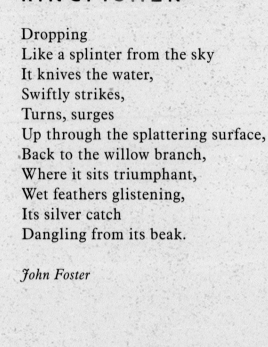

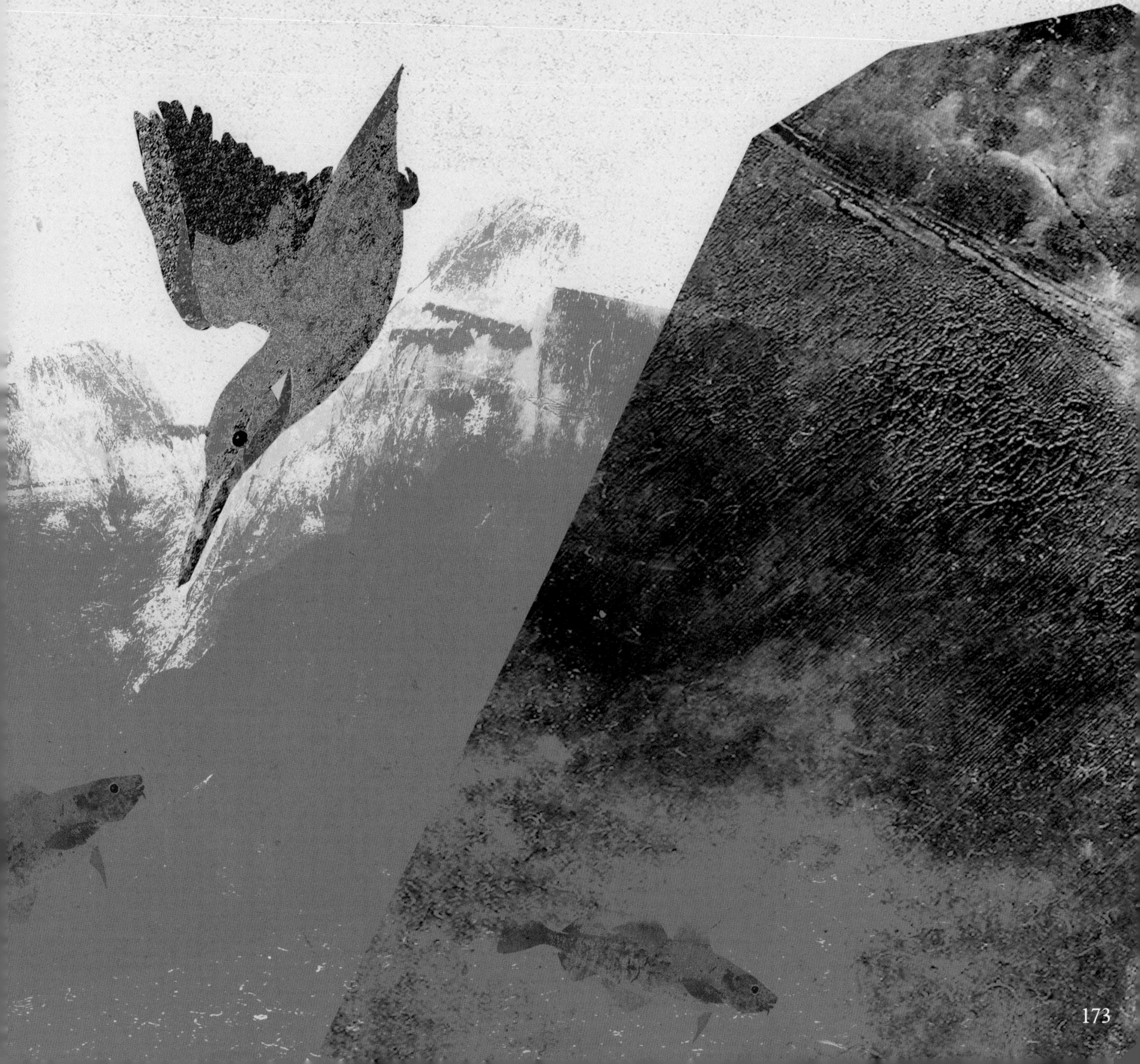

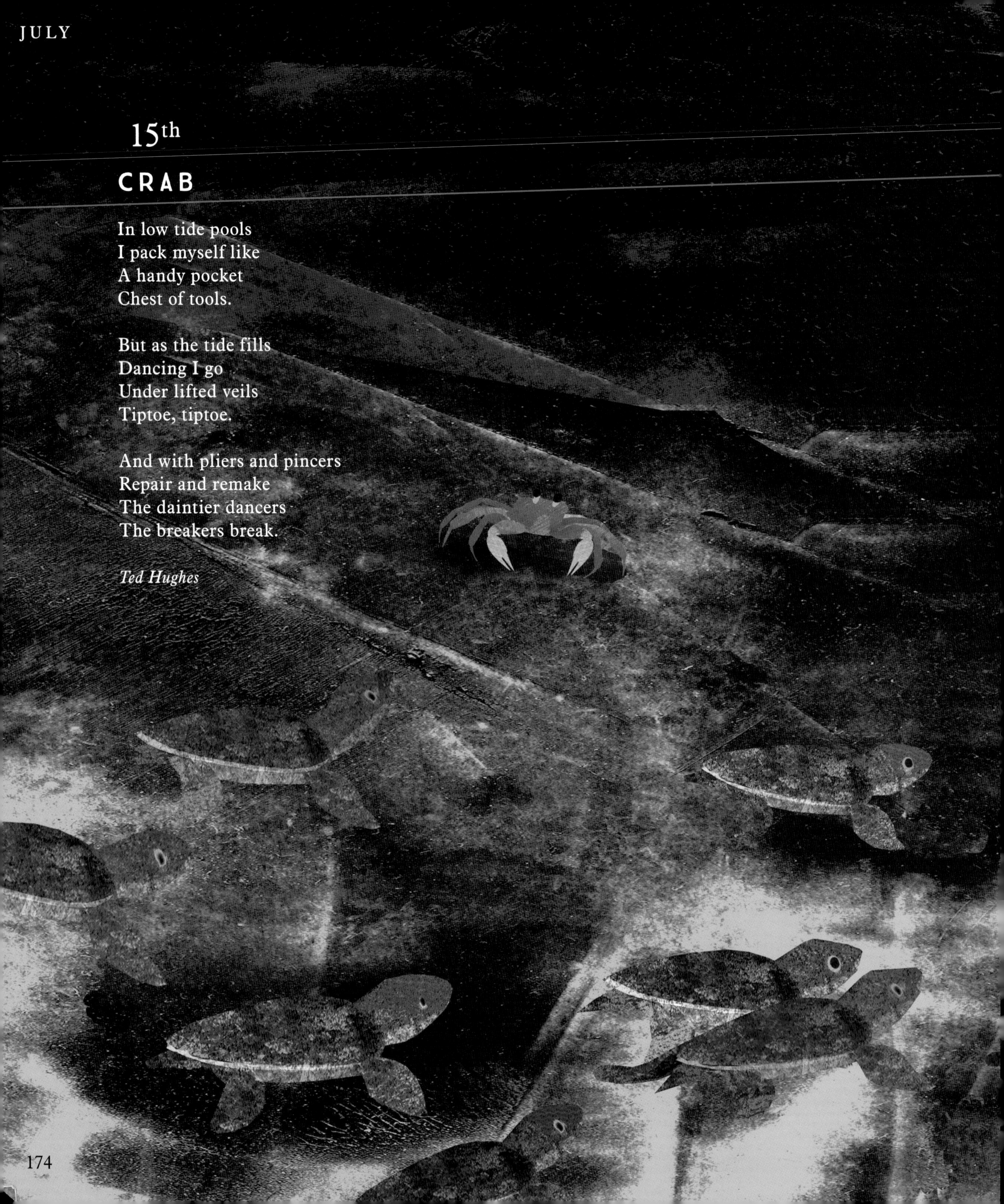

15th

CRAB

In low tide pools
I pack myself like
A handy pocket
Chest of tools.

But as the tide fills
Dancing I go
Under lifted veils
Tiptoe, tiptoe.

And with pliers and pincers
Repair and remake
The daintier dancers
The breakers break.

Ted Hughes

16th

TURTLES

When turtles hide within their shells
There is no way of knowing
Which is front and which is back
And which way which is going.

John Travers Moore

17th

OLD MOTHER TURTLE

Slow thinker
eye blinker
tank on claws
wrinkled jaws
no bigger
sand digger
risk taker
egg layer
ambles off
does not watch
her tiny hatchlings
scrape, scuffle
hurry, shuffle
down to meet
the welcoming
waves.

Patricia Leighton

18th

BUMBLEBEE

Why do you bumble?
Are you unsure what to do
in your stripy suit?

Angela Topping

19th

MUMBLING BEES

All around the garden flowers
Big velvet bees are bumbling,
They hover low and as they go
They're mumbling, mumbling, mumbling.

To lavender and snapdragons
The busy bees keep coming,
And all the busy afternoon
They're humming, humming, humming.

Inside each bell-shaped flower and rose
They busily go stumbling,
Collecting pollen all day long
And bumbling, bumbling, bumbling.

Daphne Lister

20th

BEE SONG

Bees in the late-summer sun
Drone their song
Of yellow moons
Trimming black velvet,
Droning, droning a sleepysong.

Carl Sandburg

21st

HOW DOTH THE LITTLE BUSY BEE

How doth the little busy bee
    Improve each shining hour
And gather honey all the day
    From every passing flower!

How skilfully she builds her cell;
    How neat she spreads the wax!
And labours hard to store it well
    With the sweet food she makes.

Isaac Watts

23rd

THE ELEPHAN

The elephant
Is a variant
Of a colossus
That overpowers us
By its dignity
And its ability
To avoid smashing
Life. Never dashing
Through the dense
Forests—its senses
Alert to the smallest
Vibration, blest
With the patience
Of an ancient
Queen.

Bashabi Fraser

22nd

THE GRASSHOPPER
AND THE ELEPHANT

Way down south where bananas grow
Grasshopper stepped on Elephant's toe.
Elephant said, with tears in his eyes:
"Pick on somebody your own size!"

Anonymous

24th

THE HOOPOE

A rare one with us—
King Solomon's messenger to the Queen of Sheba;
Sheltered that wise king
From the heat of the midday sun.

He offered a reward—they asked
For crowns of gold.

Poor silly birds—soon everybody harried them
With sticks and stones, until the king
Turned the gold crowns to feathers.
A feathered crown is best.

John Heath-Stubbs

25th

THE PURPOSE OF
KEEPING A TORTOISE

A tortoise
is not a pet I long to keep.
In Summer?
All he does is eat and crawl.
In Winter?
Hide and sleep!

Judith Nicholls

26th

SOLILOQUY OF A TORTOISE ON REVISITING THE LETTUCE BEDS AFTER AN INTERVAL OF ONE HOUR WHILE SUPPOSED TO BE IN A CLUMP OF BLUE HOLLYHOCKS

One cannot have enough
Of this delicious stuff!

E. V. Rieu

27th

THE MOVING HOUSE

Forever walking, carrying its home
Wherever it goes
Munching grass and leaves
It makes faces and throws
Its weight around.
The shell-sleeves
Dance with each stride.
Prowling every inch of ground
Steady in the bumpy ride
The tortoise knows where to hide.
The earth moves out of its way,
And the tortoise cools in the heat of the day.

Faustin Charles

28th

GALAHS

Several times a day
the clatter of wings
and pink and grey chatter
interrupts the quiet
just by our camp.
An old tree
leaning over the creekbed
is the place where
galahs drop by for a natter.
Mostly they don't talk long.
A quick screech, and off.
A galah's life
is one long visit.

David Homer

29th

GALAHS

There are about fifty of them
on the stony ground

some standing still
some moving about.

Nothing much of pink
breast or lighter-hued crest

shows in the twilight
among the stones.

They are standing about
like little grey-coated aldermen

talking in undertones.

William Hart-Smith

30th

THE AARDVARK

The aardvark knows a lot of things,
but seldom has been heard
to say a single syllable
much less an aardvark word.

The aardvark surely would enjoy
the chance to make a sound,
but no one pays attention
when the aardvark comes around.

To so ignore the aardvark
makes the aardvark disinclined
to join in conversation
and reveal what's on his mind.

Jack Prelutsky

31st

Ever heard
an aardvark
bark?

Miaows and birdcalls
all mill to its grist

South Africa's leading
veldtriloquist.

Roger McGough

AUGUST

1st

THE SHARK

The shark
Swims
In the dark
Of the deep
Its eye gleams
As it sees
Streams
Of gold fish—
Bold fish
Swimming too near
For the shark is well aware
That here
Is a tasty dish
Of fish
And the shark lies
In wait —
No fisherman,
No flies
No bait.
And the fish swim past
The shark follows—
Fast,
And swallows.

Leila Ward

2nd

ABOUT THE TEETH
OF SHARKS

The thing about a shark is—teeth,
One row above, one row beneath.

Now take a close look. Do you find
It has another row behind?

Still closer—here, I'll hold your hat:
Has it a third row behind that?

Now look in and . . . Look out! Oh my,
I'll *never* know now! Well, goodbye.

John Ciardi

3rd

THE BARRACUDA

Slowly, slowly he cruises,
And slowly, slowly he chooses
Which kind of fish he prefers to take this morning;
Then without warning
The Barracuda opens his jaws, teeth flashing,
And with a horrible, horrible grinding and gnashing,
Devours a hundred poor creatures and feels no remorse.
It's no wonder of course,
That he really ought, perhaps, to change his ways.
"But" (as he says
With an evil grin)
"It's actually not my fault, you see!
I've nothing to do with the tragedy;
I open my mouth for a yawn and—ah me—
They all
            swim
                    in."

John Gardner

4th

THE EAGLE

High soars the eagle

A stealthy angel in flight

Piercing eyes on all

Allyson Baker

5th

HIPPO

The hippo is a visual joke,
inflated like a rubber bed,
whose little bulging features poke
out of a yawning head.

Her jaws are built to match her girth,
with palate ribbed for emphasis.
Full-fed, she flops upon the earth
and smiles with rosy bliss.

But when she launches from the verge
to swim with curved aquatic grace,
those nostrils, eyes and ears emerge
above a hidden face—

and as by underwater bulk
you're comprehensively surveyed . . .
is hippo an ungainly hulk?
Or marvellously made?

Margaret Toms

6th
STORK

A stork will stand
On one leg all day
It's done to rest
The other they say.

Spike Milligan

7th
SPOONBILL HAIKU

The princess of birds.
Her only competition
Is her reflection.

Jane Yolen

8th

WOODLOUSE

Armoured dinosaur,
blundering through jungle grass by
dandelion-light.

Knight's headpiece, steel-hinged
orange-segment, ball-bearing,
armadillo-drop.

Pale peppercorn, pearled
eyeball; sentence without end,
my rolling full-stop.

Judith Nicholls

9th

THE SCOTTISH EARWIG

The horny goloch is an awesome beast,
    Supple and scaly;
It has two horns, and a hantle of feet,
    And a forkie tailie.

Anonymous

10th

CATERPILLAR LUNCH

Here comes Mr. Caterpillar
            Munch! Munch! Munch!
                Nibbling through
                    A leaf or two
                        for caterpillar lunch.

Kathryn Taylor

11th

LADYBIRD

Tiniest of turtles!
Your shining back
Is a shell of orange
With spots of black.

How trustingly you walk
Across this land
Of hairgrass and hollows
That is my hand.

Your small wire legs,
so frail, so thin,
Their touch is swansdown
Upon my skin.

There! break out
Your wings and fly
No tenderer creature
Beneath the sky.

Clive Sansom

193

13th

THE RATTLESNAKE

In the stony land
Near by a rock
With head erect you crawled along

Southern Paiute song,
translated by John Wesley Powell

12th

DIAMOND RATTLESNAKE

Her tough skin glistens
in the burning sunlight.
Dark raisin eyes sparkle—
fangs like curved icicles.

She traces an 'S' across the sand
leaving picture patterns.
A writhing, slithering lasso
on her slow journey to wherever.

Arching like a gymnast,
curving like a living rainbow,
no instrument can match her music.

John Rice

14th

THE VULTURE

The vulture eats between his meals
And that's the reason why,
He very, very rarely feels
As well as you or I.

His eye is dull, his head is bald,
His neck is growing thinner.
Oh! what a lesson for us all
To only eat at dinner.

Hilaire Belloc

15th

LIZARD

A lizard ran out on a rock and looked up, listening
no doubt to the sounding of the spheres.
And what a dandy fellow! The right toss of a chin for you
And swirl of a tail!

If men were as much men as lizards are lizards
they'd be worth looking at.

D. H. Lawrence

17th

BATS AT EVENING

Under the husk
        of a Scottish dusk
black bats scatter.

At high pine height
        splitting the night
they dart and clatter.

They shake the lake
        bank and brake
as the shadows shatter.

And as damp dark falls
        they cancel their calls
—a midge meal fatter!

John Rice

16th

NIGHT CREATURES

Lizards licking
crickets cricking
bats flapping
snakes slipping
owls scowl
dogs howl
chickens flurry
mongoose hurry
spiders sneaking
frogs creaking
mosquitoes sipping
rats ripping.
"GOODNIGHT!"

Pauline Stewart

18th

Even with insects—
some can sing,
        some can't.

*Kobayashi Issa,
translated by Robert Hass*

19th

MOSQUITO

Mozzie

e e
e e e
e e e
e e e e
e e e e
e e e
e e e
e
e
e e
e e e
e e e e
e e e
e e e e
e e e e
e e e e
e e e e
e e e
e e

Marie Zbierski

20th

GIRAFFES

Giraffes
  I like them.
  Ask me why.
      Because they hold their heads up high.
      Because their necks stretch to the sky.
      Because they're quiet, calm, and shy.
      Because they run so fast they fly.
      Because their eyes are velvet brown.
      Because their coats are spotted tan.
      Because they eat the tops of trees.
      Because their legs have knobby knees.
      Because
      Because
      Because. That's why
I like giraffes.

Mary Ann Hoberman

21st

GIRAFFE

Giraffe,
Sometimes
You make me laugh,
Way up there
In the skies.

But when
You stoop
To stare at me,
You cut me
Down to size.

John Foster

22nd

THE GIRAFFE

The 2 fs
in giraffe
are like
2 giraffes
running through
the word giraffe

The 2 fs
run through giraffe
like 2 giraffes

Ron Padgett

23rd

Beside the road
Mallow flowers bloom—
Now eaten by my horse!

Matsuo Bashō,
translated by Kenneth Koch

24th

THE FOUR HORSES

White Rose is a quiet horse
    For a lady to ride,
Jog-trotting on the high road
    Or through the countryside.

Grey Wolf is a hunter
    All muscle and fire;
Day long he will gallop
    And not tumble or tire.

Black Magic's a racehorse;
    She is gone like a ghost,
With the wind in her mane
    To whirl past the post.

But munching his fill
    In a field of green clover
Stands Brownie the carthorse,
    Whose labour is over.

James Reeves

26th

WREN

A tidy wren, tiny apron on,
spot-checks the garden.

Not a speck—
she's gone.

Richard Price

25th

THE BEE'S KNEES

Great hairy knees bees have as they squat
in the flowers then push off with a spring,
all six knees pumping and shoving.
With so much power they're soon airborne, resilient,
muscular, adrift.

The bee's knees.

Brilliant.

George Szirtes

27th

CRICKETS

Crickets
Talk
In the tall
Grass
All
Late summer
Long.
When
Summer
Is gone,
The dry
Grass
Whispers
Alone.

Valerie Worth

28th

SINGING

Little birds sing with their beaks
In the apple trees;
But little crickets in the grass
Are singing with their knees.

Dorothy Aldis

29th

HARVEST MOUSE

A sleek, brown acrobat, he climbs
The golden cornstalk till it sways
And sags beneath him. As it swings,
His tail-end twines a neighbour stalk
And balancing with tail and claw
He climbs aloft until he finds
The crisp, ripe, bristly ear of corn;
Then lies along its tilting length,
As if all corn-ears were created
For mice to nibble at . . . and nibbles.

Clive Sansom

30th

HAWK

The forest is the only place
where green is green and blue is blue.
Walking the forest I have seen
most everything. I've seen a you
with yellow eyes and busted wing.
And deep in the forest, no one knew.

Wendy Videlock

31st

The flying leaves
In the field at the front
Are enticing the cat.

*Kobayashi Issa,
translated by R. H. Blyth*

SEPTEMBER

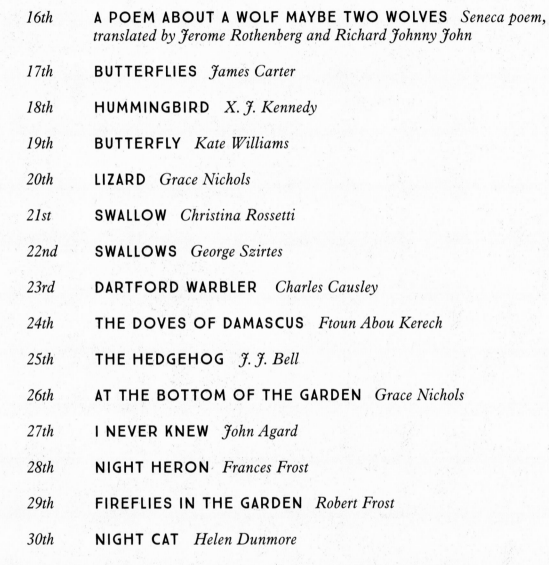

1ˢᵗ

STRIPPERS

If you fall in a river that's full of Piranha,
They'll strip off your flesh like you'd skin a banana.
There's no time for screaming, there's no time for groans.
In forty-five seconds you're nothing but bones.

Dick King-Smith

2nd

THE GUPPY

Whales have calves,
Cats have kittens,
Bears have cubs,
Bats have bittens.
Swans have cygnets,
Seals have puppies,
But guppies just have little guppies.

Ogden Nash

3rd

Half of the minnows
Within this sunlit shallow
Are not really there.

J. W. Hackett

4th

THE DUSK

A kangaroo is standing up, and dwindling like a plant
with a single bud.
Fur combed into a line
In the middle of its chest,
a bow-wave
under slanted light, out in the harbour.
And its fine unlined face is held on the cool air:
a face in which you feel
the small thrust-forward teeth lying in the lower jaw,
grass-stained and sharp.
Standing beyond a wire fence, in weeds,
against the bush that is like a wandering smoke.
Mushroom-coloured,
And its white chest, the underside of a growing mushroom,
in the last daylight.

Robert Gray

5th

KANGAROO HAIKU

Out of the forest,
on to the dry plain you spring,
light with grassy dreams.

Judith Nicholls

6th

RIDDLE

I am
pear-drop,
space-hopper,
rest-on-a-tail;
fast as a rocket,
and what's in my pocket
small as a snail?
I'm shorter than elephant,
taller than man;
I hop-step-and-jump
as no creature can.
My jacket is fur,
my pocket is too;
a joey hides there . . .
I am

(KANGAROO!)

Judith Nicholls

7th

THE MANATEE

I'm partial to the manatee,
which emanates no vanity.
It swims amidst anemones
and hasn't any enemies.

Jack Prelutsky

8th

BUFFALO DUSK

The buffaloes are gone.
And those who saw the buffaloes are gone.
Those who saw the buffaloes by thousands and how they pawed the
      prairie sod into dust with their hoofs, their great heads down
      pawing on in a great pageant of dusk,
Those who saw the buffaloes are gone.
And the buffaloes are gone.

Carl Sandburg

9th

THE FLOWER-FED BUFFALOES

The flower-fed buffaloes of the spring
In the days of long ago,
Ranged where the locomotives sing
And the prairie flowers lie low;
The tossing, blooming, perfumed grass
Is swept away by wheat,
Wheels and wheels and wheels spin by
In the spring that still is sweet.
But the flower-fed buffaloes of the spring
Left us long ago.
They gore no more, they bellow no more,
They trundle around the hills no more:
With the Blackfeet, lying low,
With the Pawnees, lying low.

Vachel Lindsay

10th

CHANT TO THE FIREFLY

Firefly, firefly, light me to bed.
Come, come, little insect of light,
You are my candle, and light me to go.

Anishinaabe song,
translated by Henry Rowe Schoolcraft

11th

"I've seen everything,
Right to the bottom of the pond"—
The look on the duckling's face.

Naitō Jōsō,
translated by Geoffrey Bownas and Anthony Thwaite

12th

I'M A YELLOW-BILL DUCK

I'm a yellow-bill duck
with a black feather back,
I waddle waddle waddle,
And I quack quack quack!

I dabble for my dinner
with a swish swish swish,
and I gobble gobble gobble
all I wish wish wish!

Jack Prelutsky

14th

BLACK SWAN

On one leg
I feel the deep-earth cool,
the slide of an inch of water
before it drops, white in sun sparks,
and I swan-dream of a summer
of days like this; my hard red mouth
in the down of my feathers, black
as anthracite gathering heat
from a distant star.

Graham Burchell

13th

SWIM, SWAN!

Swan swam over the sea,
    Swim, swan, swim!
Swan swam back again,
Well swum, swan!

Anonymous

15th

WOLF

Mine is the howl
that chills the spine
in the forest gloom;
mine is the whine.

Mine is the nose
that breathes in fear
when danger's close;
mine is the ear.

Mine is the fur
the huntsmen trade;
mine is the fur,
I am afraid.

Judith Nicholls

16th

A POEM ABOUT A WOLF MAYBE TWO WOLVES

Y
  o
    w
      e
        e
          e

he comes running
across the field where   e
he comes running   e
        e
      e
    e
  e
        he comes running
y   across the field where
  o   he comes running
    w
      e
        e
          e
            e
              e

Seneca poem,
translated by Jerome Rothenberg
and Richard Johnny John

17th

BUTTERFLIES

Those showy-offy butterflies
really aren't so very wise

Who cares if they've got pretty wings?
butterflies are s n o o t y things

James Carter

18th

HUMMINGBIRD

Cried a scientist watching this creature dart by,
"Why, its wings are too small for it! How dare it fly?"
So he figured and figured and finally found
That it just couldn't possibly get off the ground,

And they made him Professor. But still, hummingbird
Kept on flying to flower beds. It hadn't heard.

X. J. Kennedy

19th

BUTTERFLY

On wings flake-fragile,
petal-frail, you somehow sail,
mile after long mile.

Kate Williams

20th

LIZARD

A lean wizard—
watch me slither
up and down
the breadfruit tree
sometimes pausing a while
for a dither in the sunshine

The only thing
that puts a jitter up my spine
is when I think about
my great great great
great great great great
great great grandmother
Dinosaura Diplodocus

She would have the shock of her life
if she were to come back
and see me reduced to lizardsize!

Grace Nichols

21ˢᵗ

SWALLOW

Fly away, fly away over the sea,
Sun-loving swallow, for summer is done;
Come again, come again, come back to me,
Bringing the summer and bringing the sun.

Christina Rossetti

22ⁿᵈ

SWALLOWS

Hunting on the wing
all billow and swoop
laughing as they go
pouring from the sky
in one vast troupe
they fly tails forked
suddenly uncorked

George Szirtes

23rd

DARTFORD WARBLER

Stay-at-home
    Never-roam
        Dartford warbler
Hiding in furze
    On the yellow plain,
        Skulking in scrub,
Secret in heather
    As seasons turn
        And turn again;

Spending your day
    On the highest spray
        Or sprig or twig
Where you first
    Saw day;
        Wearing the English
Storm and summer,
    Never, ever
        To fly away.

Restless, hole-in-
    The-corner creeper,
        I watch in spring
When you bob
    Like a ball
        High on the bush-top
Singing, scattering
    Rattling music
        Over all.

Slate-wing, starveling
    Beyond my window,
        Cheery, unweary
In sun, in snow,
    Packed my bag
        I hear you crying,
"You too! You too!
    Tell me, spell me
        Why do you go?"

Charles Causley

24th

THE DOVES OF DAMASCUS

I lost my country and everything I had before.
and now
I cannot remember for sure

the soft of the snow in my country,
I cannot remember
the feel of the damp air in summer.

Sometimes I think I remember
the smell of jasmine
as I walked down the street.

And sometimes autumn
with its orange and scarlet leaves
flying in the high Damascus sky.

And I am sure I remember
my grandmother's roof-garden,
its vines, its sweet red grapes,

the mint she grew in crates for tea.
I remember the birds, the doves
of Damascus. I remember

how they scattered.
I remember
trying to catch them.

Ftoun Abou Kerech

25th

THE HEDGEHOG

The Hedgehog sleeps beneath the hedge—
    As you may sometimes see—
And I prefer it sleeping there
    To sleeping here with me!

J. J. Bell

26th

AT THE BOTTOM OF THE GARDEN

No, it isn't an old football
grown all shrunken and prickly
because it was left out so long
at the bottom of the garden.

It's only Miss Hedgehog
who, when she thinks I'm not looking,
unballs herself to move . . .
    like bristling black lightning.

Grace Nichols

27th

I NEVER KNEW

I never knew
a crown of thorns
could curl itself
into a ball

I never knew
a hairbrush
could breathe in
and out

I never knew
a nest of needles
could sprout
a beady nose
and actually move

Not until I lifted
that old carpet
beside the garden shed
and met HEDGEHOG
my bristling brother.

John Agard

28th

NIGHT HERON

Hunting my cat along the evening brook
Where she'd been stalking deer mice in the weeds,
I nearly missed this sight—the great night heron
Bluer than dusk in the maze of willow reeds.

Beautiful, motionless, he stood in silence
On one leg, waiting for lantern flies,
And gazed across the brook to where in hemlock
His nest of sticks rose high against the skies.

Then at my feet I saw my fierce young hunter
Crouched in the wet grass, trembling and in awe.
We left our heron to his stars. Cat shivered
And touched my cheek with a damp and golden paw.

Frances Frost

30th

NIGHT CAT

She's there by the fence
but you mustn't call out,
like a scoop of night
or a water shadow
tense for flight
she'll twist and go,
don't open your mouth—
the moon's so close
that the stars blow out—
you turn   she's gone
leaving that patch
where the moon shone
leaving the empty
dress of night
with the stars picked out
and you alone.

Helen Dunmore

29th

FIREFLIES IN THE GARDEN

Here come real stars to fill the upper skies,
And here on earth come emulating flies,
That though they never equal stars in size,
(And they were never really stars at heart)
Achieve at times a very star-like start.
Only, of course, they can't sustain the part.

Robert Frost

OCTOBER

1st

THE SPARROW HAWK

Wings like pistols flashing at his sides,
Masked, above the meadow runway rides,
Galloping, galloping with an easy rein.
Below, the fieldmouse, where the shadow glides,
Holds fast the small purse of his life, and hides.

Russell Hoban

2nd

THE WUZZY WASPS
OF WASPERTON
(EXTRACT)

The wuzzy wasps of Wasperton
Are buzzing round the pears
And choosing all the ripe ones—
They think the orchard's theirs.

Daphne Lister

3rd

THE WASP

When the ripe pears droop heavily,
The yellow wasp hums loud and long
His hot and drowsy summer song.
A yellow flame he seems to be,
When darting suddenly from high
He lights where fallen peaches lie.

Yellow and black—this tiny thing's
A tiger soul on elfin wings.

William Sharp

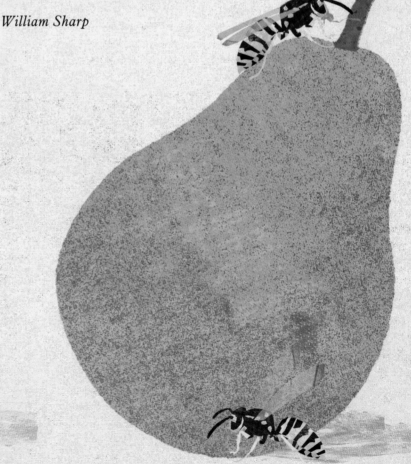

4th

THE WASP

Help me to love the wasp,
help me to do that thing—
to admire the raspy buzz
of its wings, to grow fond
of its droning whinge.

Help me to clasp the wasp
to my breast, or at least
to train it to jump from my finger
to thumb, a stripy pet,
to get it to fetch, to stand up

and beg, waving two of its six
little legs, to play dead. Help me
to like the passionate kiss
of its sting, to do that thing.
Help me to love the wasp.

Carol Ann Duffy

5th

WASPS

Wasps in brightly
Coloured vests,
Chewing wood,
To make their nests.

Wasps, like rockets,
Zooming high,
Then dropping down
Where peaches lie.

Anne Ruddick

6th

BUTTERFLY

Butterfly
Butterflies
Butterflown

Michael Harrison

7th

SQUIRREL

The squirrel in the hickory tree's a
nervous fellow,
all quiver and scurry.
See him

hurl himself upon
a limb
worry a nut
pack his cheeks
race
downtree
to a secret place and
hurry
back
in furry frenzy.

There's something he knows
that makes him
go,
this soft slow
mellow
autumn day.

It has to do with
hunger
in the snow.

Lilian Moore

8th

SQUIRRELS

Tails like dandelion clocks
They blow away, these
Lightweight bucking broncos
With a plume behind.

For sheer surprise
No well-aimed burdock
Sticks more nimbly to your overcoat
Than these to tree bark,

Nor with such aplomb
Can any comparable creature
Lead a dance more deftly
Through the branches.

Down to earth again, they
Hold their tums in, little aldermen,
Or sit on tree stumps
Like old ladies knitting socks.

John Mole

9th

SPIDER

With what voice,
And what song would you sing, spider,
In this autumn breeze?

Matsuo Bashō,
translated by Kenneth Koch

10th

PARROTS

Loquats are cold as winter suns.
Among rough leaves their clusters glow
like oval beads of cloudy amber
or small fat flames of birthday candles.

Parrots, when winter dwindles
their forest fruits and seeds, remember
where the swelling loquats grow,
how chill and sweet their thin juice runs;

and shivering in the morning cold
we draw the curtains back, and see
the lovely greed of their descending,
the lilt of flight that blurs their glories

and warm our eyes upon the lories
and the rainbow-parrots landing.
There's not a fruit on any tree
can match their crimson, green and gold.

To see them cling and sip and play
loquats are no great price to pay.

Judith Wright

11th

parrots
with vermilion bands and beak
green-iris camouflaging
are acrobats
swinging on trapezes of green gum leaves
tips

they carry their very own safety net
their green-yellow tail feathers
which spray out like palm fronds
parachuting

Neil Paech

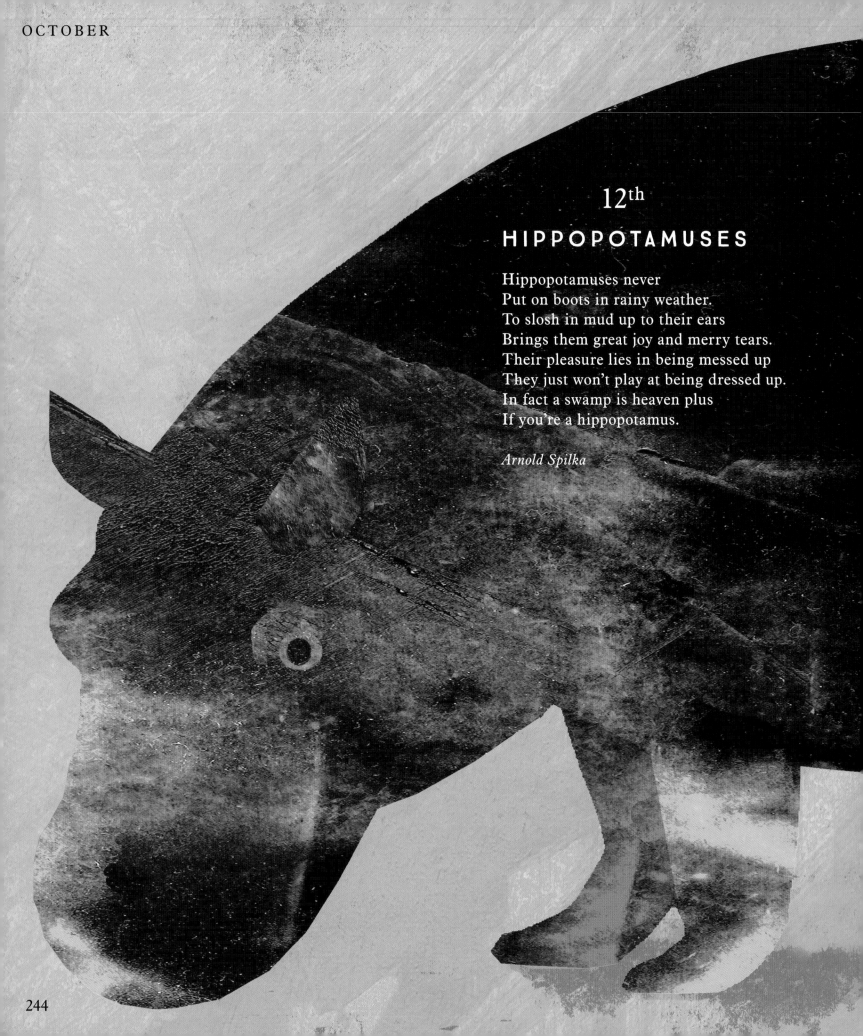

12th

HIPPOPOTAMUSES

Hippopotamuses never
Put on boots in rainy weather.
To slosh in mud up to their ears
Brings them great joy and merry tears.
Their pleasure lies in being messed up
They just won't play at being dressed up.
In fact a swamp is heaven plus
If you're a hippopotamus.

Arnold Spilka

13th

THE HIPPOPOTAMUS

The huge hippopotamus hasn't a hair
on the back of his wrinkly hide;
he carries the bulk of his prominent hulk
rather loosely assembled inside.

The huge hippopotamus lives without care
at a low philosophical pace,
as he wades in the mud with a thump and a thud
and a permanent grin on his face.

Jack Prelutsky

14th

BESIDE THE LINE OF ELEPHANTS

I think they had no pattern
        When they cut out the elephant's skin;
Some places it needs letting out,
        And others, taking in.

Edna Becker

15th

THE WORLD IS FULL OF ELEPHANTS

The world is full of Elephants,
The baby ones and taller ones.
African Elephants have great big ears,
The Indian ones have smaller ones.

Gavin Ewart

16th

ELEPHANT

ELEPHANT

The word is too heavy
to lift   too cumbersome to
lead through a room filled with
relatives or small
glass trinkets

ELEPHANT

He must have invented it
himself. This is a lumbering
gray word   the ears of it
are huge and flap like loose
wings   a word with
wrinkled knees and toes
like boxing gloves

This word   ELEPHANT
sways toward us   bulk
and skull-bones filling up
the space   trumpeting
its own wide name
through its nose!

Barbara Esbensen

17th

A dog sleeping
At the door of an empty house,
Leaves of the willow-trees scattering.

Masaoka Shiki,
translated by R. H. Blyth

18th

PLEASANT THINGS
(EXTRACT)

'Tis sweet to hear the watchdog's honest bark
Bay deep-mouth'd welcome as we draw near home;
'Tis sweet to know there is an eye will mark
Our coming, and look brighter when we come.

Lord Byron

19th

WOLF

As the muffled evening settles
moonlight pours across the floor
something in the shadows flickers
instinct lifts his grizzled jaw.

Gazing at the cloudless heavens
he sings the notes of distant stars
the songs his fathers have forgotten
beyond a world of streets and cars.

Lilting notes of coursing rivers
mournful cries on empty moors
steaming footfalls in the darkness
the garden wolf is tame no more.

Daylight often finds him yawning
or softly padding across the floor
tenderly he'll rise to greet you
then whimper by the kitchen door.

Sue Hardy-Dawson

20th

THE SHARK

He seemed to know the harbour,
So leisurely he swam;
His fin,
Like a piece of sheet-iron,
Three-cornered,
And with knife-edge,
Stirred not a bubble
As it moved
With its baseline on the water.

His body was tubular
And tapered
And smoke-blue,
And as he passed the wharf
He turned,
And snapped at a flatfish
That was dead and floating.
And I saw the flash of a white throat,
And a double row of white teeth,
And eyes of metallic grey,
Hard and narrow and slit.

Then out of the harbour,
With that three-cornered fin,
Shearing without a bubble the water
Lithely,
Leisurely,
He swam—
That strange fish,
Tubular, tapered, smoke-blue,
Part vulture, part wolf,
Part neither—for his blood was cold.

E. J. Pratt

21st

THE CORMORANT

A lone black crag stands offshore,
Lashed by the flying spray. Gorged from his fishing-foray
With long hooked beak and greenish glistering eye,
A cormorant, like a heraldic bird,
Spreads out dark wings, two tattered flags, to dry.

John Heath-Stubbs

22nd

a moment between
lighthouse flashes
cold smell of fish

David Cobb

23rd

PELICAN

Aloof   long-nosed conjurer
impeccably out of style   watch him
he will show you the neat trick
of eating.

Dip and glide   another fish pocketed
in the deep box of his bill.

He lifts extendable wings
they are empty.
He points with a cold eye
summons his mate.   They preen
practise sawing each other
in half.

Caroline Caddy

24th

THE PELICAN

The sunset glows
Like the inside of a peach
I see a pelican
Standing on the beach

The pelican looks
So clumsy and sad
I want to take him home
To my mum and dad

But he shakes his long beak
And jumps into the skies
And graceful as an angel
Away he flies

Adrian Mitchell

25th

THE PELICAN CHORUS
(EXTRACT)

Ploffskin, Pluffskin, pelican jee!
We think no Birds so happy as we!
Plumpskin, Ploshkin, Pelican jill!
We think so then, and we thought so still!

Edward Lear

26th

GREY GEESE

All night they flew over in skeins.
I heard their wrangling far away
Went out once to look for them, long after midnight.
Saw them silvered by the moonlight, like waves,
Flagging south, jagged and tired,
Across the sleeping farms and the autumn rivers
To the late fields of autumn.

Even in a city I have heard them
Their noise like the rusty wheel of a bicycle;
I have looked up from among the drum of engines
To find them in the sky
A broken arrowhead turning south
Heading for home.

The Iceland summer, the long light
Has run like rivers through their wings,
Strengthened the sinews of their flight
Over the whole ocean, till at last they circle,
straggle down on the chosen runway of their field.

They come back
To the same place, the same day, without fail;
Precision instruments, a compass
Somewhere deep in their souls.

Kenneth C. Steven

27th

GREY GOOSE AND GANDER

Grey goose and gander,
    Waft your wings together,
And carry the good king's daughter
    Over the one strand river.

Anonymous

28th

SOMETHING TOLD
THE WILD GEESE

Something told the wild geese
It was time to go.
Though the fields lay golden
Something whispered, "Snow."
Leaves were green and stirring,
Berries, luster-glossed,
But beneath warm feathers
Something cautioned, "Frost."
All the sagging orchards
Steamed with amber spice,
But each wild breast stiffened
At remembered ice.
Something told the wild geese
It was time to fly—
Summer sun was on their wings,
Winter in their cry.

Rachel Field

29th

FIVE LITTLE BEARS

One little bear
Wondering what to do
Along came another
Then there were two!

Two little bears
Climbing up a tree
Along came another
Then there were three!

Three little bears
Ate an apple core
Along came another
Then there were four!

Four little honey bears
Found honey in a hive
Along came another
Then there were five!

Anonymous

30th

THE APPLE DON'T FALL FAR FROM THE TREE

amidst . . . apple tree
black bear . . . pounces limb
cubs wait . . . below

Katherine Stella

31st

BATS

A bat is born
Naked and blind and pale.
His mother makes a pocket of her tail
And catches him. He clings to her long fur
By his thumbs and toes and teeth.
And then the mother dances through the night
Doubling and looping, soaring, somersaulting—
Her baby hangs on underneath.
All night, in happiness, she hunts and flies.
Her high sharp cries
Like shining needlepoints of sound
Go out into the night and, echoing back,
Tell her what they have touched.
She hears how far it is, how big it is,
Which way it's going:
She lives by hearing.
The mother eats the moths and gnats she catches
In full flight; in full flight
The mother drinks the water of the pond
She skims across. Her baby hangs on tight.
Her baby drinks the milk she makes him
In moonlight or starlight, in mid-air.
Their single shadow, printed on the moon
Or fluttering across the stars,
Whirls on all night; at daybreak
The tired mother flaps home to her rafter.
The others all are there.
They hang themselves up by their toes,
They wrap themselves in their brown wings.
Bunched upside-down, they sleep in air.
Their sharp ears, their sharp teeth, their quick sharp faces
Are dull and slow and mild.
All the bright day, as the mother sleeps,
She folds her wings about her sleeping child.

Randall Jarrell

NOVEMBER

1ˢᵗ

COCK-CROW

Out of the wood of thoughts that grows by night
To be cut down by the sharp axe of light, —
Out of the night, two cocks together crow,
Cleaving the darkness with a silver blow:
And bright before my eyes twin trumpeters stand,
Heralds of splendour, one at either hand,
Each facing each as in a coat of arms:
The milkers lace their boots up at the farms.

Edward Thomas

2ⁿᵈ

A bantam rooster
spreading his ruff of feathers
thinks he's a lion!

Enomoto Kikaku,
translated by Alice Behn Goebel

3rd

A PICTURE OF THE ROOSTER

A crimson comb untrimmed on the head,
All in white, a rooster walks nearby.
In his life seldom a single sound he's made,
But thousands of doors soon open to his cry.

Tang Yin

4th

A COCK CAN CROW

A cock can crow, but a crow can't cock.
A macaw can't caw but it sure can squawk.
Let a mockingbird mock at the call of an auk
but a caw's the law when crows talk.

JonArno Lawson

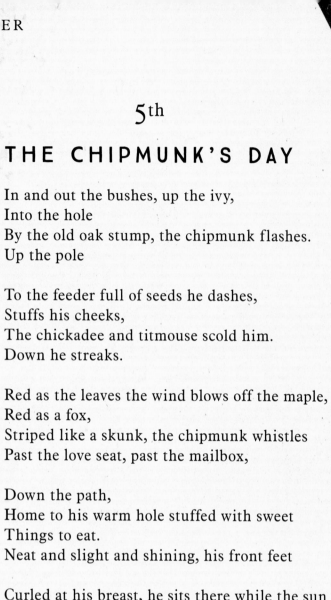

5th

THE CHIPMUNK'S DAY

In and out the bushes, up the ivy,
Into the hole
By the old oak stump, the chipmunk flashes.
Up the pole

To the feeder full of seeds he dashes,
Stuffs his cheeks,
The chickadee and titmouse scold him.
Down he streaks.

Red as the leaves the wind blows off the maple,
Red as a fox,
Striped like a skunk, the chipmunk whistles
Past the love seat, past the mailbox,

Down the path,
Home to his warm hole stuffed with sweet
Things to eat.
Neat and slight and shining, his front feet

Curled at his breast, he sits there while the sun
Stripes the red west
With its last light: the chipmunk
Dives to his rest.

Randall Jarrell

6th

LITTLE CHARLIE CHIPMUNK

Little Charlie Chipmunk was a talker!
    Mercy me!
He chattered after breakfast
    and he chattered after tea!

He chattered to his father
    and he chattered to his mother!
He chattered to his sister
    and he chattered to his brother!

He chattered 'til his family
    was almost driven wild!
Oh, little Charlie Chipmunk
    was a *very* tiresome child!

Helen Cowles LeCron

7th

THE SLOTH

In moving-slow he has no Peer.
You ask him something in his ear;
He thinks about it for a Year;

And, then, before he says a Word
There, upside down (unlike a Bird)
He will assume that you have Heard—

A most Ex-as-per-at-ing Lug.
But should you call his manner Smug,
He'll sigh and give his Branch a Hug;

Then off again to Sleep he goes,
Still swaying gently by his Toes,
And you just *know* he knows he knows.

Theodore Roethke

8th

THE BOA

Allow me just one short remark
    About this lengthy Boa:
If Noah had it in his ark,
    I sympathize with Noah!

J. J. Bell

9th

THE SLOTH

The sloth may smile,
The sloth may frown.
It's hard to tell—
he's upside down!

Colin West

10th

DOG

Asleep he wheezes at his ease.
He only wakes to scratch his fleas.

He hogs the fire, he bakes his head
As if it were a loaf of bread.

He's just a sack of snoring dog.
You can lug him like a log.

You can roll him with your foot.
He'll stay snoring where he's put.

Take him out for exercise
He'll roll in cowclap up to his eyes.

He will not race, he will not romp.
He saves his strength for gobble and chomp.

He'll work as hard as you could wish
Emptying the dinner dish.

Then flops flat, and digs down deep,
Like a miner, into sleep.

Ted Hughes

11th

CRAB DANCE

Play moonlight
and the red crabs dance
their scuttle-foot dance
on the mud-packed beach

Play moonlight
and the red crabs dance
their side-ways dance
to the soft-sea beat

Play moonlight
and the red crabs dance
their bulb-eye dance
their last crab dance

Grace Nichols

12th

CATS

Cats sleep
Anywhere,
Any table,
Any chair,
Top of piano,
Window ledge,
In the middle,
On the edge,
Open drawer,
Empty shoe,
Anybody's
Lap will do,
Fitted in a
Cardboard box,
In the cupboard
With your frocks—
Anywhere!
They don't care!
Cats sleep
Anywhere.

Eleanor Farjeon

13th

LULLABY OF A WOMAN OF THE MOUNTAINS

House, be still, and ye little grey mice,
Lie close tonight in your hidden lairs.

Moths on the window, fold your wings,
Little black chafers, silence your humming.

Plover and curlew, fly not over my house,
Do not speak, wild barnacle, passing over the mountain.

Things of the mountain that wake in the night-time,
Do not stir tonight till the daylight whitens!

Pádraic Pearse

14th

My first is in mud but not in bog,
My second's in wood and also in log.
My third is in yours, but not in mine,
My fourth is in sun, and also in shine.
My fifth is in here, and also in there,
And when you're not around I run everywhere.
What am I?

[A mouse]

Anonymous

15th

M was once a little mouse.
    Mousy,
    Bousy,
    Sousy,
    Mousy.
In the housy,
    Little mouse!

Edward Lear

16th

the sound of the bat
flying in the thicket
is dark.

*Masaoka Shiki,
translated by R. H. Blyth*

17th

NOVEMBER HARE

The November hare
is neither here nor there.

As the cold squeezes in
it is where it's been

though it's hard to know where.

George Szirtes

18th

monochrome fellow
making tunnels in the soil
dusk adventurer

Simon Hodge

19th

AESTHETIC CURIOSITY

Does an owl appreciate
The color of leaves
As they fall about him
In the staggering nights of Autumn?

A. M. Klein

20th

THE WOLF

When the pale moon hides and the wild wind wails,
And over the treetops the nighthawk sails,
The gray wolf sits on the world's far rim,
And howls: and it seems to comfort him.

The wolf is a lonely soul, you see,
No beast in the wood, nor bird in the tree,
But shuns his path; in the windy gloom
They give him plenty, and plenty of room.

So he sits with his long, lean face to the sky
Watching the ragged clouds go by.
There in the night, alone, apart,
Singing the song of his lone, wild heart.

Far away, on the world's dark rim
He howls, and it seems to comfort him.

Georgia Roberts Durston

21st

A WOLF...

A wolf
I considered myself
but
the owls are hooting
and
the night I fear.

*Teton Sioux song,
translated by Robert P. Higheagle,
recorded by Two Shields,
collected by Frances Densmore*

22nd

THE OWL SPEAKS

Evening is growing red.
Straight above me the color
spreads out in all directions.
I fly out and hoot at it
Four times.

Papago song,
translated by Ruth Murray Underhill

23rd

EGGS

Eggs are laid by turkeys
Eggs are laid by hens
Eggs are laid by robins
Eggs are laid by wrens
Eggs are laid by eagles
Eggs are laid by quail,
Pigeons, parrots, peregrines:
And that's how every bird begins.

Mary Ann Hoberman

24th

TO BE ANSWERED
IN OUR NEXT ISSUE

When a great tree falls
And people aren't near,
Does it make a noise
If no one can hear?
And which came first,
The hen or the egg?
This impractical question
We ask and then beg.
Some wise men say
It's beyond their ken.
Did anyone ever
Ask the hen?

Anonymous

25th

The chicken wants
To say something—
Fidgeting its feet.

Karai Senryū,
translated by Geoffrey Bownas and Anthony Thwaite

26th

The turkey was back
this time bringing all his friends
to wander the woods

Anonymous

279

27th

MY SONG
(EXTRACT)

> I sing the ocean
> with wading birds and gulls in constant motion.
> My song is of the summer's early light
> of winter's wind and rain at dark midnight.

Robin Fry

28th

DAY OUT

Walking on a low cliff edge,
We watched two seals at sea.
We stared at them—they stared at us,
with expressions of curiosity.
They disappeared and reappeared,
seemed to follow us for a mile or two,
and very soon we began to wonder
just who was watching who.
Perhaps it was *their* day out
and we were exhibits
in their zoo.

Nigel Gray

29th

the plovers of the shore
played about
wetting their feet

Yosa Buson,
translated by R. H. Blyth

30th

WHISPER TO ME

Whisper to me while the spider spins,
sing me a song of seagulls' wings,
tell me the story of sky and hill,
put me to sleep in a pāua shell.

Kōhimuhimu mai he rangirangi pūngāwerewere,
waiatatia he oriori parirau karoro,
kōrerotia mai he pūrākau a Rangi, a Nuku,
kia pai ai taku moe i rō anga pāua.

Patricia Grace

DECEMBER

1st

DO THE SNUFFAROUND

I got a yellow dog
Watch her for hours
She snuffles with her snout
Around the trees and flowers

She snuffs at the grass
She sniffs at the ground
Then she starts digging
Like a natural hound

She does The Snuffaround
She does The Snuffaround
She uses paws and jaws
And claws because
She loves The Snuffaround

Well she lowers her head
Snuffles at the grime
Then her tail starts wagging
In double time

She holds up one paw
Shoves down her snout
Gonna dig those moles
And rabbits out

She does The Snuffaround
She does The Snuffaround
She uses paws and jaws
Like there ain't no laws
She loves The Snuffaround

She digs with the left paw
Digs with the right
Digs with both together
She'll be digging all night

She's kicking back earth
Mud clay and sand
She won't stop digging
Till Kangarooland

She does The Snuffaround
She does The Snuffaround
She uses paws and jaws
Doesn't stop for applause
And that's The Snuffaround

Adrian Mitchell

2nd

DOGS

The dogs I know
Have many shapes
For some are big and tall,
    And some are long,
        And
        some
        are thin,
And some are fat and small.
And some are little bits of fluff
And have no shape at all.

Marchette Chute

3rd

STARLINGS

How they startle the air
with the wings of their flair

Grace Nichols

4th

THE MANEUVER

I saw the two starlings
coming in toward the wires.
But at the last,
just before alighting, they

turned in the air together
and landed backwards!
that's what got me—to
face into the wind's teeth.

William Carlos Williams

5th

MURMURATION
(EXTRACT)

The starlings lean
like woodsmoke on the fields
and blow away.

Jean Atkin

6th

IT IS I, THE LITTLE OWL

Who is it up there on top of the lodge?
Who is it up there on top of the lodge?
    It is I,
    The little owl,
    coming down—
    It is I,
    The little owl,
    coming down—
    coming down—
    down—
    coming
    down—
    down—

Who is it whose eyes are shining up there?
Who is it whose eyes are shining up there?
    It is I,
    The little owl,
    coming down—
    It is I,
    The little owl,
    coming down—
    coming—
    down—
    coming
    down—
    down—

Chippewa poem,
translator unknown

7th

WHAT SEES THE OWL
(EXTRACT)

His velvet wing sweeps through the night;
With magic of his wondrous sight
He oversees his vast domain,
And king supreme of night doth reign.

Elizabeth Sears Bates Gerberding

8th

Crow on the fence,
Rain will go hence.
Crow on the ground,
Rain will come down.

Anonymous

9th

A MEMORY

This I remember,
I saw from a train
A shaggy wild pony
That stood in the rain.

Where I was going,
And where was the train,
I cannot remember,
I cannot explain.

All these years after
It comes back again:
A shaggy wild pony
That stood in the rain.

Douglas Gibson

10th

ON A NIGHT OF SNOW

Cat, if you go outdoors you must walk in the snow,
You will come back with little white shoes on your feet,
Little white slippers of snow that have heels of sleet.
Stay by the fire, my Cat. Lie still, do not go.
See how the flames are leaping and hissing low,
I will bring you a saucer of milk like a marguerite,
So white and so smooth, so spherical and so sweet—
Stay with me, Cat. Outdoors the wild winds blow.

Outdoors the wild winds blow, Mistress, and dark is the night.
Strange voices cry in the trees, intoning strange lore,
And more than cats move, lit by our eyes' green light,
On silent feet where the meadow grasses hang hoar—
Mistress, there are portents abroad of magic and might,
And things that are yet to be done. Open the door!

Elizabeth Coatsworth

11th

CAT IN THE DARK

Mother, Mother, what was that?
Hush, my darling! Only the cat.
(Fighty-bitey, ever-so-mighty)
Out in the moony dark.

Mother, Mother, what was that?
Hush, my darling! Only the cat.
(Prowly-yowly, sleepy-creepy,
Fighty-bitey, ever-so-mighty)
Out in the moony dark.

Mother, Mother, what was that?
Hush, my darling! Only the cat.
(Sneaky-peeky, cosy-dozy,
Prowly-yowly, sleepy-creepy,
Fighty-bitey, ever-so-mighty)
Out in the moony dark.

Mother, Mother, what was that?
Hush, my darling! Only the cat.
(Patchy-scratchy, furry-purry,
Sneaky-peeky, cosy-dozy,
Prowly-yowly, sleepy-creepy,
Fighty-bitey, ever-so-mighty)
Out in the moony dark.

Margaret Mahy

12th

THE PANDA

You're a bamboo bandit;
you're a piebald dream.
You're a bear in silk pajamas;
you're cookies and cream.
You're the wizard of the mountains;
you're pres-ti-di-gi-ta-tion!
You're nature's best example
of bear imagination.

David Elliott

13th

THE SCOTTISH WILDCAT

She scuffs paw prints in fresh snow—blunted, shallow;
a low-slung sun burnishing her bridging back.
Heads north, ranging over a netherworld,
tasting salt in the air as she slopes towards a drab sea.

It is a wide land: once plenteous, now tightfisted—
this is no courteous domain, no gallant land.
And this windswept shoreline will offer no abundance.
Behind, there is clamour, voices raised, tempers taut.

Almond-eyed, she surveys left, right and ahead.
A salted, north-tethered wind dampens her nostrils:
amid the clamour of gulls and the slash of waves,
she turns, raises her head to the sun, defiantly,
and pads back to her forest kin.

John Rice

14th

I'VE NEWS FOR YOU

I've news for you
the stag bellows,
winter's snow,
summer's gone,

high cold wind,
sun low in sky,
short days,
heavy seas,

deep red bracken's
skeletal form,
barnacle goose's
customed call,

cold has seized
the bird's wings,
icy season:
that's my news.

Anonymous,
translated by Seán Hutton

15th

THE PTARMIGAN

The ptarmigan is very odd,
As odd as odd can be.
It never sits on a ptelegraph pole
Or roosts up in a ptree
And pto spell his name
You have pto put
A "p" before the "t"!

Anonymous

16th

WHALES WEEP NOT!
(EXTRACT)

All the whales in the wider deeps, hot are they, as they urge
on and on, and dive beneath the icebergs.
The right whales, the sperm whales, the hammerheads, the killers
there they blow, there they blow, hot wild white breath out of the sea!

D. H. Lawrence

17th

WHALE

Wouldn't you like to be a whale
And sail serenely by—
An eighty-foot whale from the tip of your tail
And a tiny, briny eye?
Wouldn't you like to wallow
Where nobody says "Come out!"
      Wouldn't you *love* to swallow
      And blow all the brine about?
Wouldn't you like to be always clean
But never to have to wash, I mean,
And wouldn't you love to spout—
      O yes, just think—
A feather of spray as you sail away,
And rise and sink and rise and sink,
And blow all the brine about?

Geoffrey Dearmer

18th

YAK

The yak—the yak
Will rarely attack
It's a docile little beast
Will not harm you in the least.

Spike Milligan

19th

THE YAK

Yickity-yackity, yickity-yak,
the yak has a scriffily, scraffily back;
some yaks are brown yaks and some yaks are black,
yickity-yackity, yickity-yak.

Sniggildy-snaggildy, sniggildy-snag,
the yak is all covered with shiggildy-shag;
he walks with a ziggildy-zaggildy-zag,
sniggildy-snaggildy, sniggildy-snag.

Yickity-yackity, yickity-yak,
the yak has a scriffily, scraffily back;
some yaks are brown and some yaks are black,
yickity-yackity, yickity-yak.

Jack Prelutsky

20th

SNOW FOX

In the Arctic summer
the cloud-grey fox
listens for prey
in the low shrubs and rocks

grizzled and still
as the permafrost ground
his senses vivid
with scent and sound

when lemmings are hidden
under the snow
the wild geese are flown
and biting winds blow

a horizon-less white
shrouds the Arctic fox
in clouds of snow fur
from tail-tip to socks

he haunts frozen sea
as thin as the air
hoping for scraps
missed by polar bear

or curls in his tail
from the star-cold white
chewing on hunger
through long Arctic night

and waits for spring sun
and pale Arctic day
to melt tundra snow
and his white coat away

Liz Brownlee

21st

THE ARCTIC FOX

No feet. Snow.
Ear—a star-cut
Ache of air
The world hangs watched.

Jaws flimsy as ice
Champ at the hoar-frost
Of something tasteless—
A snowflake of feathers.

The forest sighs.
A fur of breath
Empty as moonlight
Has a blue shadow.

A dream twitches
The sleeping face
Of the snow-lit land.

When day wakes
Sun will not find
What night hardly noticed.

Ted Hughes

22nd

SONG OF THE LEMMING

On a cold winter's day, a little lemming came out of his warm hole.
He looked about him, shivered, shook himself, and sang:

> The sky,
> like a vast belly,
> arches itself
> around my burrow.
> The air is clear,
> no clouds in sight:
> icy weather! Aiee!
> I'm freezing! freezing!

Inuit song,
collected by Knud Rasmussen
and translated by Tom Lowenstein

23rd

ARCTIC VIXEN

The snowfox
the winter fox

is the colour
of bushy snow

her breath
like a white brush

and her eye
rusty.

Michael Baldwin

303

24th

THE OXEN

Christmas Eve, and twelve of the clock.
  "Now they are all on their knees,"
An elder said as we sat in a flock
  By the embers in hearthside ease.

We pictured the meek mild creatures where
  They dwelt in their strawy pen,
Nor did it occur to one of us there
  To doubt they were kneeling then.

So fair a fancy few would weave
  In these years! Yet, I feel,
If someone said on Christmas Eve,
  "Come; see the oxen kneel

"In the lonely barton by yonder coomb
  Our childhood used to know,"
I should go with him in the gloom,
  Hoping it might be so.

Thomas Hardy

25th

THE DONKEY

I saw a donkey
      One day old,
His head was too big
      For his neck to hold;
His legs were shaky
      And long and loose,
They rocked and staggered
      And weren't much use.
He tried to gambol
      And frisk a bit,
But he wasn't quite sure
      Of the trick of it.
His queer little coat
      Was soft and gray
And curled at his neck
      In a lovely way.
His face was wistful
      And left no doubt
That he felt life needed
      Some thinking about.
So he blundered round
      In venturesome quest,
And then lay flat
      On the ground to rest.
He looked so little
      And weak and slim,
I prayed the world
      Might be good to him.

Gertrude Hind

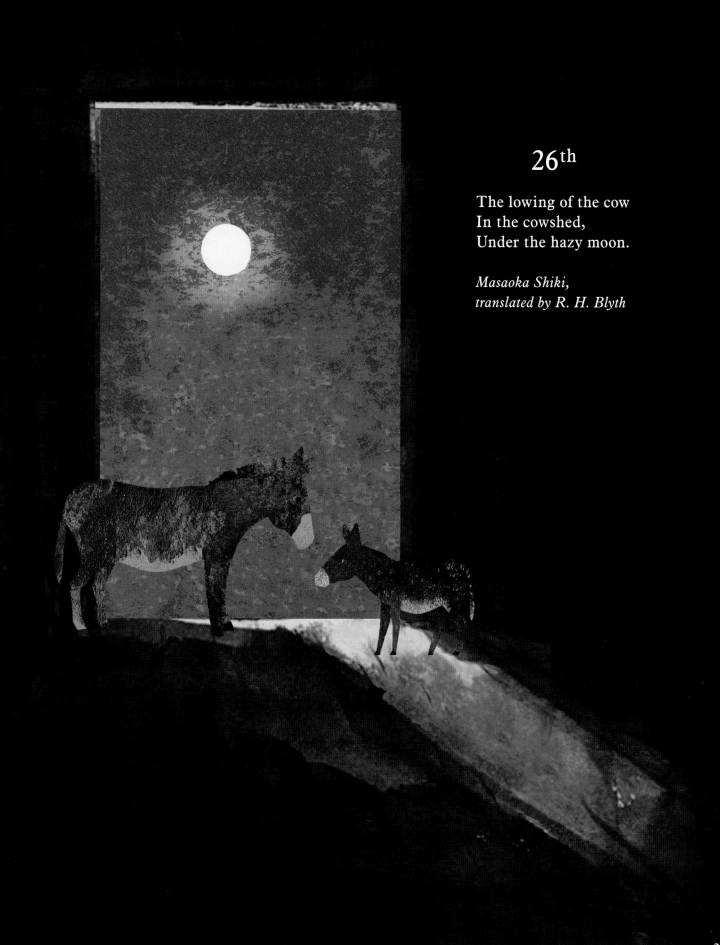

26th

The lowing of the cow
In the cowshed,
Under the hazy moon.

Masaoka Shiki,
translated by R. H. Blyth

27th

THE POLAR BEAR

The polar bear by being white
gives up his camouflage at night,
And yet, without a thought or care,
he wanders here, meanders there,
and gaily treads the icy floes
completely unconcerned with foes.
For after dark nobody dares
to set out after polar bears.

Jack Prelutsky

28th

PENGUINS

The penguins' habitat is freezing—
You'll like it there
If you don't mind sneezing,
(I, myself, don't find it pleasing.)

Helen H. Moore

29th

PENGUIN

Perfectly equipped for swimming, streamlined in
Every detail, see him speed through the water,
Notice how on land, he waddles like an old-fashioned
Gentleman going in to dinner,
Up and down he goes, flat-footed, slow. But
In the water he
Never looks absurd, this graceful, polar, water-bird.

June Crebbin

30th

SNOW PETRELS

On skies and seas
veiled white with light,
snow petrels weave
and wheel in flight,

they glide and skim
from high to low,
a falling flock
of feathered snow.

In courtship chases
pair by pair
they braid their paths
of freezing air,

birds of Antarctic
paradise,
the cliffs, the sea,
the snow, the ice.

Liz Brownlee

31st

WORD

The word bites like a fish.
Shall I throw it back free
Arrowing to that sea
Where thoughts lash tail and fin?
Or shall I pull it in
To rhyme upon a dish?

Stephen Spender

INDEX OF POETS

INDEX OF POEMS

INDEX OF FIRST LINES

ACKNOWLEDGEMENTS

John Agard: "Flying Fish" copyright © John Agard 2002, "Hippo Writes a Love Poem to His Wife" copyright © John Agard 1996, "I Never Knew" copyright © John Agard 1992, "Laughter's Favourite Animal" copyright © John Agard 1990 and "Woodpecker" copyright © John Agard 1984, reproduced by kind permission of John Agard c/o Caroline Sheldon Literary Agency Ltd. **Dorothy Aldis:** "Every Insect" by Dorothy Aldis, illustrated by Peggy Westphal, copyright © 1960 by Dorothy Aldis, renewed; from *Quick as a Wink GB* by Dorothy Aldis; "Singing", copyright © 1925–1927, renewed 1953, © 1954, 1955 by Dorothy Aldis; from *Everything and Anything* by Dorothy Aldis; used by permission of G. P. Putnam's Sons Books for Young Readers, an imprint of Penguin Young Readers Group, a division of Penguin Random House LLC. All rights reserved. **Laura Allen:** "The Horse" from *Wondercrump Poetry 3* by Children for Children. Published by Red Fox. Reprinted by permission of The Random House Group Limited. © 1996. **Giles Andreae:** "Chimpanzee" from *Rumble in the Jungle*, copyright © Giles Andreae, first published in the UK by Orchard Books, an imprint of Hachette Children's Group, Carmelite House, 50 Victoria Embankment, London, EC4Y 0DZ. **Moira Andrew:** "Zebra" from *How to Turn Your Teacher Purple* compiled by James Carter, A&C Black 2011, copyright © Moira Andrew, reprinted by permission of the author. **Joan Walsh Anglund:** "Ladybug" from *Morning is a Little Child*, Harcourt, Brace & World Inc 1969, copyright © Joan Walsh Anglund 1969, reprinted in arrangement with the Rita Rosenkranz Literary Agency. **Jean Atkin:** "The starlings lean" is an extract from "Murmuration", which was first published in *Not Lost Since Last Time* (Oversteps Books, 2013). Reprinted by permission of the author. **Mary Austin:** "Grizzly Bear" from *The Children Sing in the Far West* by Mary Austin. Copyright © 1928 by Mary Austin, renewed 1956 by Kenneth M. Chapman and Mary C. Wheelwright. Reprinted by permission of Houghton Mifflin Harcourt Publishing Company. All rights reserved. **Allyson Baker:** "The Eagle", Wattpad.com: Ally_B24, copyright © Allyson Baker 2020, reprinted by permission of the author. **Michael Baldwin:** "The Small Brown Bear" from *Poetry for Pleasure* compiled by RK Sadler and TAS Hayllar, Macmillan Education AU Pty Ltd 1991; "Arctic Vixen" from *A First Poetry Book* compiled by John Foster, Oxford University Press 1979; copyright holders unknown. **Matsuo Bashō:** (UK) "Beside the road" and "Spider" from *Talking to the Sun*, Kenneth Koch and Kate Farrell, Holt Rinehart and Winston 1985, English translation by Kenneth Koch based on the word-for-word translation by Harold Henderson in *An Introduction to Haiku*. Reprinted by permission of the Kenneth Koch Literary Estate. (US & Canada) "Beside the road" and "Spider" from *Talking to the Sun: An Illustrated Anthology of Poems for Young People* © 1985 by Kenneth Koch and Kate Farrell. Reprinted by permission of Henry Holt Books for Young Readers. All Rights Reserved. **Edna Becker:** "Beside the Line of Elephants" from *Pickpocket Songs*, The Caxton Printers Ltd 1935, copyright © Edna Becker, reprinted by permission of Bonnie Becker Beelman. **Hilaire Belloc:** "The Scorpion" and "The Vulture" from *Complete Verse* by Hilaire Belloc, reprinted by permission of Peters Fraser & Dunlop (www.petersfraserdunlop.com) on behalf of the Estate of Hilaire Belloc. **Ronald M. Berndt:** "Paddling, we saw that turtle", reproduced with permission of Buku-Larrnggay Mulka Centre on behalf of Rirratjiŋu clan, Yolŋu people, North East Arnhem Land, Northern Territory, Australia. Translation reproduced courtesy Estate of the late Catherine H. Berndt. Originally published in Berndt, R. M. (1952) *Djanggawul: An Aboriginal Religious Cult of North-Eastern Arnhem Land*. London: Routledge (p.64). **Nozawa Bonchō:** "In a shimmer of air" by Nozawa Bonchō from *The Monkey's Straw Raincoat, and Other Poetry of the Bashō School* by Earl Miner and Hiroko Odagari, Princeton University Press 1981, reprinted by permission of Erik Miner. **Margaret Wise Brown:** Poetry selections titled: "Green Stems" and "Wild Black Crows" from *Nibble Nibble* by Margaret Wise Brown. Text copyright © 1959 by William R. Scott, Inc. Renewed 1987 by Roberta Brown Rauch. Used by permission of HarperCollins Publishers. **Sandy Brownjohn:** "Roll Play" from *In and Out of the Shadows*, Oxford University Press 2000, text copyright © Sandy Brownjohn 2000, reproduced with permission of the Licensor through PLSclear. **Liz Brownlee:** "Bat Words" first published at Bristol Zoo 2007, copyright © Liz Brownlee 2007; "An Elephant is Born" and "Snow Petrels" from *Shouting at the Ocean: Poems that Make a Splash* edited by Graham Denton, Roger Stevens and Andrea Shavick, Hands Up Books 2009, copyright © Liz Brownlee 2009; "Hedgehog Hugs" from *The Jumble Book* edited by Roger Stevens, Macmillan Children's Books 2009, copyright © Liz Brownlee 2009; "Snow Fox" from *Poetry for a Change: A National Poetry Day Anthology*, Otter-Barry Books 2018, copyright © Liz Brownlee 2018; reprinted by permission of the author. **Graham Burchell:** "Black Swan" from *The RSPB Anthology of Wildlife Poetry* compiled by Celia Warren, A&C Black 2011, copyright © Graham Burchell 2011, reprinted by permission of the author. **Caroline Caddy:** "Pelican" by Caroline Caddy, from *Letters from the North*, copyright © 1985, published by Fremantle Press, Western Australia, reprinted with permission. **James Carter:** "Butterflies" from *Hey, Little Bug!* Frances Lincoln Children's Books 2011, copyright © James Carter 2011, reprinted by permission of the author. **Lucy-Beth Cassidy:** "Snow Leopard Haiku" from write4fun.net 2017, reprinted by permission of the author. **Charles Causley:** "Dartford Warbler" from *I Had a Little Cat: Collected Poems for Children*, Macmillan Children's Books 1996, copyright © Charles Causley, reprinted by permission of David Higham Associates. **Faustin Charles:** "Light in the Night", "The Moving House" and "Platypus" from *Once Upon an Animal*, Bloomsbury Publishing 1998, copyright © Faustin Charles, reprinted by permission of the author. **Marchette Chute:** "Dogs" from *Around and About*, EP Dutton 1957, copyright © Marchette Chute, reprinted by permission of Elizabeth Weinrich. **John Ciardi:** "About the Teeth of Sharks" from *You Read to Me, I'll Read to You*, HarperCollins Publishers, copyright © John Ciardi, reprinted by permission of the Ciardi Publishing Trust, John L. Ciardi, Trustee. **Leonard Clark:** "Miracle" from *The Corn Growing*, Hodder Children's Books 1982, copyright © Leonard Clark 1982, reprinted by permission of The Literary Executor of Leonard Clark. **Jane Clarke:** "Porcupine Valentine" from *Wacky Wild Animals* chosen by Brian Moses, Macmillan Children's Books 2000, copyright © Jane Clarke 2000, reprinted by permission of the author. **Elizabeth Coatsworth:** "March" from *Summer Green* (Macmillan & Co. 1948); "On a Night of Snow" from *Nine Lives* (Andre Deutsch 1977); "Song of the Rabbits Outside the Tavern" from *Country Poems* (Macmillan 1942); reprinted by permission of The Marsh Agency Ltd on behalf of © The Estate of Elizabeth Coatsworth. **David Cobb:** "A moment between" from *The Iron Book of British Haiku*, Iron Press 1998, copyright © David Cobb, reprinted by permission of the author. **Paul Cookson:** "Who Am I? (A kenning)" from *A First Poetry Book* edited by Pie Corbett and Gaby Morgan, Macmillan Children's Books 2012, copyright © Paul Cookson 2012, reprinted by permission of the author. **Frances Cornford:** Extract from "A Child's Dream" from *Selected Poems*, Enitharmon Press 1996, copyright © Frances Cornford, reproduced with the permission of the trustees of the Frances Crofts Cornford Will Trust. **June Crebbin:** "Penguin" from *The Dinosaur's Dinner*, Puffin Books 1992, copyright © June Crebbin, reprinted by permission of the author. **Jennifer Curry:** "City Bees" from *Down Our Street* by Jennifer Curry. Published by Methuen, 1988. Copyright © Jennifer Curry. Reproduced by permission of the author c/o Rogers, Coleridge & White Ltd., 20 Powis Mews, London W11 1JN. **Ruth Dallas:** "A Fly" from *Shadow Show* by Ruth Dallas, Caxton Press 1968, reprinted by permission of Joan Dutton. **Adele Davide:** "Hare" by Adele Davide, from *A Footprint in the Air* compiled by Naomi Lewis, Hutchinson 1983, copyright © Adele Davide, reprinted by permission of the author. **Roberta Davis:** "Perfectly still" from *The Iron Book of British Haiku*, Iron Press 1992, copyright © Roberta Davis, reprinted by permission of the author. **Carmen Bernos de Gasztold:** "Prayer of the Butterfly" from *Prayers from the Ark*. Translation copyright © Rumer Godden 1962. Reproduced with permission of Curtis Brown Group Ltd, London, on behalf of The Beneficiaries of the Estate of Rumer Godden. **Jan Dean:** "Grey Wolf" and "Mole" from *The Penguin in Lost Property*, Macmillan Children's Books 2014, copyright © Jan Dean 2014, reprinted by permission of the author. **Geoffrey Dearmer:** "Whale" from *Down in the Marvellous Deep*, Orchard Books 1994, copyright © Geoffrey Dearmer, reprinted by permission of Juliet Woollcombe. **Frances Densmore:** "A Wolf" Teton Sioux song, recorded by Two Shields, translated by Robert P. Higheagle, collected by Frances Densmore in *Teton Sioux Music and Culture*, University of Nebraska Press 2001. **Emily Dickinson:** "A narrow fellow in the grass" from *The Poems of Emily Dickinson: Variorum Edition*, edited by Ralph W. Franklin, Cambridge, Mass.: The Belknap Press of Harvard University Press. Copyright © 1998 by the President and Fellows of Harvard College. Copyright © 1951, 1955 by the President and Fellows of Harvard College. Copyright © renewed 1979, 1983 by the President and Fellows of Harvard College. Copyright © 1914, 1918, 1919, 1924, 1929, 1930, 1932, 1935, 1937, 1942 by Martha Dickinson Bianchi. Copyright © 1952, 1957, 1958, 1963, 1965 by Mary L. Hampson. **Carol Ann Duffy:** "The Wasp" from *New and Collected Poems for Children* by Carol Ann Duffy. Published by Faber & Faber, 2009. Copyright © Carol Ann Duffy. Reproduced by permission of the author c/o Rogers, Coleridge & White Ltd., 20 Powis Mews, London W11 1JN. **Helen Dunmore:** "Baby Orangutan" from *A Poem for Every Night of the Year*, edited by Allie Esiri, Macmillan Children's Books 2016, copyright © Helen Dunmore; "Night Cat" from *Secrets: A Collection of Poems from Hidden Words*, Bodley Head Children's Books 1994, copyright © Helen Dunmore 1994; reproduced with permission of The Estate of Helen Dunmore. www.bloodaxebooks.com. **Richard Edwards:** "Awake, Asleep" and "The Anaconda" from *Teaching the Parrot*, Faber and Faber 1996, copyright © Richard Edwards 1996, reprinted by permission of Faber and Faber Ltd. **David Elliott:** "The Panda" and "The Lion" from *In the Wild*. Copyright © 2010 David Elliott. Reproduced by permission of the publisher, Candlewick Press, Somerville, MA. **Gavin Ewart:** "The World is Full of Elephants" and "The Meerkats of Africa" from *Caterpillar Stew: A Feast of Animal Poems*, Hutchinson 1990, copyright © Gavin Ewart, reprinted by permission of the Estate of Gavin Ewart. **U. A. Fanthorpe:** "The Sheepdog" from U. A. Fanthorpe, *New and Collected Poems*, Enitharmon, 2010, reprinted by permission of Dr R V Bailey. **Eleanor Farjeon:** "Cats" from *Blackbird Has Spoken*, Macmillan Children's Books 1999, copyright © Eleanor Farjeon, reprinted by permission of David Higham Associates. **Aileen Fisher:** "Baby Chick" from *Always Wondering* by Aileen Fisher. Text Copyright © 1991 by Aileen Fisher. All Rights Renewed and Reserved. Reprinted by permission of Marian Reiner on behalf of the Boulder Public Library Foundation, Inc. **Michael Flanders:** "The Hummingbird" from *All Creatures Great and Small*, Holt, Rinehart and Winston 1965, copyright © Michael Flanders 1965, reprinted by permission of the Michael Flanders Estate. **John Foster:** "Kingfisher" copyright © 2008 John Foster, from *The Poetry Chest* (Oxford University Press), and "Giraffe" copyright © 1987 John Foster, from *Another First Poetry Book* (Oxford University Press), included by permission of the author. **Bashabi Fraser:** "The Elephant" from *Rainbow World*, Hodder Children's Books 2003, copyright © Bashabi Fraser, reprinted by permission of the author. **Frances Frost:** "Night Heron" from *The Little Naturalist*, McGraw-Hill 1959, copyright © 2019 by Joan Blackburn, reprinted by permission of Joan Blackburn. **Robert Frost:** (UK) "Fireflies in the Garden" from *The Poetry of Robert Frost* by Robert Frost. Published by Jonathan Cape. Reprinted by permission of The Random House Group Limited. © 1972. (US & Canada) "Fireflies in the Garden" by Robert Frost from the book *The Poetry of Robert Frost* edited by Edward Connery Lathem. Copyright © 1928, 1969 by Henry Holt and Company. Copyright © 1956 by Robert Frost. Reprinted by permission of Henry Holt and Company. All rights reserved. **Robin Fry:** Extract from "My Song" from *Love Song of the Wading Bird*, Makaro Press 2014, reprinted by